LIFE IS WAR

LIFE IS WAR

Surviving Dictatorship in Communist Albania

Shannon Woodcock

HammerOn Press

In this engaging and moving book, Shannon Woodcock provides English-language audiences with a rare and often brutal portrait of the Communist rule of Enver Hoxha (1944-1985), through her careful recording of the memories of ordinary Albanians who lived through 'that time'. From poor peasants and workers, to people with 'bad biographies', the book's subjects recount, with often excruciating detail, the dreams and lives that were crushed, and also the small but significant ways some of them defied the regime. As one woman puts it: these are stories 'that could make you laugh and cry at the same time'. In the best tradition of oral histories of dictatorship, Woodcock highlights the ruthlessness of state repression, the intimacies brought about not just by solidarity, but also by mistrust and enmity. But she also conveys the importance of jokes and humour as modes of survival, the power of which endures through memory in the form of what the author aptly calls 'retrospective rebellion'. As well as a study of violence, trauma and remembering, this is a powerful book about the intensity, intimacy and imagination of story telling. The tales of twenty-first century Albanians blends with astute historical commentary and accounts of contemporary life in one of Europe's poorest nations. Woodcock's detailed descriptions of her impressions during two years traveling through the country leave the reader with a vivid picture of the Albanian landscape - and also of the enduring legacy of dictatorship and hardship in the lives and struggles of people today.

Carrie Hamilton, Reader in History, University of Roehampton.

This book is one of those rare works that combines that best of two worlds, academia and literature. The book is rigorously academic in its investigation, analysis as well as the insights it offers. At the same time it

reads like a novel that you cannot put down. Through moving individual life stories Woodcock allows the reader to peer into and understand everyday life in a totalitarian system. Hence, these are not the stories of some isolated and random individuals. They are carefully chosen and detailed accounts of individual struggles, suffering and survivals that sum up the life of a whole nation under an oppressive communist regime.

Its combination of academic rigour and literary skill sets this book apart from other works on communist Albania in particular and communism in general. As an academic work the book throws a unique and penetrative gaze on everyday life in communist Albania. One of its many academic merits here is that it dispels socially held notions in Albania about the strong rule of law under communism, as opposed to a lawless transition period, by disclosing how in everyday life Albanians experienced state power as highly arbitrary and unpredictable. As a literary work the book is unparalleled in its redemptive character as far as the victims of Albanian communism are concerned. Through the act of narration this book redeems the stories and lives of its characters, which would have otherwise perished in oblivion. One can hardly ask more of a book.

Blendi Kajsiu, Faculty of Law and Political Science, University of Antioquia, Colombia.

Life is War gives voice to the experiences of Albanians—men, women, Romani, Vlachs among them—who survived Enver Hoxha's notoriously repressive and increasingly isolated regime. The stories Shannon Woodcock chronicles enrich our limited knowledge of everyday life in Albania, and are a welcome addition to social histories and collected memory studies of the communist period in Eastern Europe.

Gail Kligman, co-author of the award-winning *Peasants Under Siege: The Collectivization of Romanian Agriculture, 1949-1962.*

LIFE IS WAR: SURVIVING DICTATORSHIP
IN COMMUNIST ALBANIA
© Shannon Woodcock, 2016

ISBN-13: 978-1-910849-03-3
ISBN-10: 1910849033

H A M M E R / O N

Life is War: Surviving Dictatorship in Communist Albania/
Shannon Woodcock
1. Communist Studies 2. Albania 3. Trauma Studies
4. East European History 5. 20th Century Social History
6. Oral History 7. Romani Studies 8. Gender Studies

First published in 2016 by HammerOn Press
Bristol, England
http://hammeronpress.net

Cover design and typeset by Eva Megias
http://evamegias.com

Contents

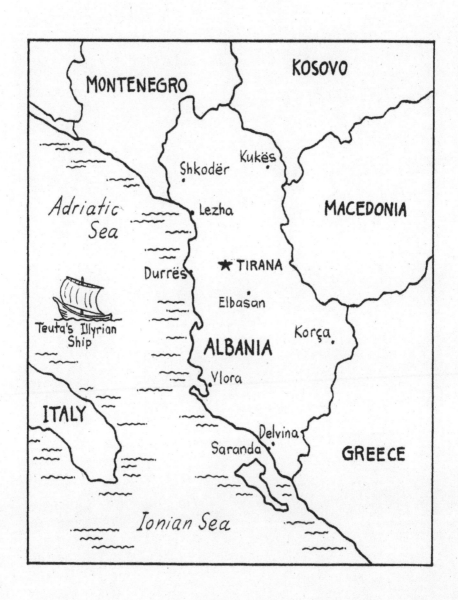

Introduction

The grandmother of my friend sat beside me on the floral print couch while her daughters cooked Sunday lunch. My friend had left me here, at his aunt's house, while he went for coffee with his uncles. When the old woman asked me who I was, I replied in Albanian that I was an Australian historian who lived in Tirana.

"Can I trust her?" she called out to her daughters.
"Trust her! Who can she report to nowadays?" one called back.

The old woman, neatly dressed with carefully pinned, long, grey hair, looked into my eyes. "I've had five daughters," she began. "All of them were born here in Durres, as I was. After the war the communists called us enemies of the people and I was put to work. I was fourteen. The prisoners were mixed together; men and women, criminals and political prisoners. We worked draining the marshes, and I only had one dress. I had to wash it in the sea when it was dirtied. The men and women worked and slept all mixed together. Do you understand me? I only had one dress."

She paused, her brown eyes fixed on mine. I nodded. "*Kuptoj*. I understand." She pulled herself up off the couch and shuffled away down the corridor. One of her daughters came out of the kitchen, wiping her hands on a towel. "Oh no, now she's crying again," she said, looking in the direction her mother had taken. I was alarmed. I'd been a historian in Romania and Albania since 1997, had spoken to survivors and perpetrators of atrocities, and was attentive to whether people became upset or not in telling me their stories. The old woman had chosen to speak to me – she knew I understood what she was telling me, and she had seemed serious, not upset. Nevertheless, I wondered if I had made a mistake. Then she shuffled back into the living room again, holding a stack of photo albums in her small hands. She sat on the couch and gestured to me to come and sit beside her.

She began her story again, from the beginning. Her father and his father had been businessmen since the Albanian state was declared in 1912 and through the interwar years of monarchy rule. When the communists came to power in 1944, they confiscated the family's house and her father's vast library, sending the books that were not banned to stock the new public libraries. Every time she came close to breaking down – when she spoke of the communists taking her family to forced labour as state enemies after World War Two, although she was only a child, or of the decades of persecution until 1991 – she opened the albums and told me the names of her present day family members, photographed at weddings and celebrations. She would bring herself back from the memories of persecution by touching the images of the loved ones around her. She was not just teaching me about the past, but how she had survived it.

After that moment in 2009 I began to record people's memories of everyday life in Albania between 1944 and 1991, the period of Communist Party rule. For many, such as this woman, the story began before 1944, when Enver Hoxha came to power. Ethnic Albanian statesmen had declared Albania a nation in 1912 in the wake of the fallen Ottoman Empire. Invaded by Italy in World War One, the independent successive Albanian governments between the first and second World Wars failed to ameliorate the poverty in Albania's population of less than a million people. Albanians in the mountainous north spoke what became known as the Gheg dialect, while southern Albanians spoke the Tosk dialect. Very few people owned more than small parcels of land, and a minority of the population was literate. The Kingdom of Albania, ruled by King Zog was established in 1925, but struggled to raise enough funds from the few who had wealth to develop infrastructure or make pervasive changes to the accessibility of education. Interwar Albania was a new nation in which, as in Romania, many passionate individuals worked hard to create higher standards of living not just for their own families but for their communities.

In 1939, Italy invaded Albania and World War Two began. Germany moved through Albania to invade Greece in 1941, and the Nazis occupied Albania after Italy withdrew in 1943. Many Albanians resisted Italian and German occupation by becoming partisans with one of three groups that fought for Albanian independence; the Communist Party, *Balli Kombëtar* (nationalist movement), or *Legaliteti*, supporters of King Zog's Albanian monarchy. In 1944 Enver Hoxha led the Communist Party of Albania into Tirana and claimed the liberation and rule of Albania. Hoxha ruled until his death in 1985. The Communist Party changed its name in 1948 to the Party of Labor of Albania (*Partia e Punës e Shqipërisë, PPSH,* in Albanian), and was the only legal political party. I refer to the Party of Labor of Albania as "the Party" throughout this book.

Throughout the four decades of his rule, Hoxha led Albania through splits with the socialist governments of Yugoslavia (1948), the Soviet Union (1955-1961) and finally with the last of their allies, China (1978). With each political split, Hoxha denounced his former comrades as revisionists, purging vast numbers of his own Party members and their families, from ministers down to low level bureaucrats. Punishments included execution, prison, and internment, which meant being sent to a regional city or village to live under surveillance.

As soon as Hoxha came to power he attacked the clergy of Albania's three religious groups (Roman Catholicism, Orthodox Christianity and Islam) and pre-communist politicians, intellectuals, businessmen and members of the *Balli Kombëtar*. After 1956 Hoxha purged people with educational, political or ethnic ties to the USSR, and in the 1960s he implemented the Albanian version of Mao Zedong's Cultural Revolution, declaring war against all religion and superstition. In the early 1970s,

Hoxha attacked "cultural imperialism" and purged people working in the arts, the television stations, and cultural fields, as well as individuals accused of certain styles of dress and behaviour. After 1978, Hoxha maintained the nation as a paranoid and isolated state, convincing the people that both the West and East could invade at any moment.

Through the 1980s, Albanians became poorer than ever. Production of glass, fertilizer, paints, steel and chemicals slowed and stopped without support from China to the small mountainous nation. The Party ensured that everyone's time was fully occupied with work, compulsory military training, compulsory voluntary work, and queuing to get enough food to feed one's family. From 1967, when Hoxha called for "the emancipation of women," women had to work both at home and in the public sphere. Thus women were "emancipated" to the bulk of the housework, and to the same gruelling schedule as men in the workforce (six days a week) as well as compulsory military service and "voluntary" labour.

I lived in Romania before I arrived in Albania, and I knew how oppressive Ceaușescu's dictatorship had been. Hoxha's Albania, however, was more internationally isolated than Ceaușescu's Romania, and Albania's much smaller population enabled a strikingly higher degree of regime surveillance and control. The Romanian population was almost 16 million in 1950 compared with 1.2 million in Albania, and there were 22 million Romanians by 1989, and just 3.2 million Albanians. Throughout the duration of the regimes, the Albanian state persecuted a higher percentage of their population than the Romanian state persecuted in Romania. The Albanian Directorate of State Security, the *Sigurimi*, employed a higher percentage of the Albanian population than the percentage of the Romanian population employed by the *Securitatea* in Romania. The Albanian Party waged a constant war to divide and conquer within families and communities; most people you will meet in this book believed and experienced that the Party persecuted at least one person in each family.

In 1990 there were approximately 40,000 people in forced labour camps throughout Albania and 26,000 people in jails. The Party killed thousands throughout the decades with execution, imprisonment and forced labour. Tens of thousands more were sent to live in internal exile, under surveillance and shunned, in villages across Albania.

From the small population, a proportionately small number of people were Party elites. Party Politburo members and Enver Hoxha lived in the centre of Tirana in an area the size of a few city blocks, called "the block." The armed guards at the entrance to the block prevented any public access, and there were few who dared approach without permission. Everyone else in Albania lived mixed together; those with "good biographies" (*biografi të mirë*, referring to an unblemished political record in the eyes of the Party), alongside those with "bad biographies" (*biografi të keq*), those who were "enemies of the people" (meaning enemies of the proletariat) in the "class war" of socialist ideology. People with bad biographies may have been accused of a political crime, or have relatives who had fled Albania, or relatives who had been purged for ideological (religious, political, or class) reasons. In various places, political prisoners were used for labour in the cooperative fields neighbouring those where free people worked.

Having the proletariat living and working alongside those named "enemies of the people" kept everyone under control. Those with good biographies had examples of the cost of a "stain" to one's biography before their eyes every day, and they also had to participate in socially and professionally excluding people with bad biographies. Associating with an "enemy of the people" could stain one's biography, and so those with good biographies usually didn't befriend, socialise, or marry into families that had a bad biography. Everyone knew that paid *Sigurimi* informers were everywhere because so many people were approached by the *Sigurimi* and invited to make some money themselves. Denunciations for far-fetched and fabricated crimes led to public trials, and some of the convicted were executed at night in accessible places around the countryside. Enemies of the state were sometimes executed by public hanging. The bodies of thousands of people murdered by the regime remain unaccounted for today.

Hoxha's paranoid isolationist policies were renowned even within the sphere of European communist dictatorships. In fact, when I mentioned to research contacts in the Romanian military that I had moved to Tirana, I discovered that Albania had been the outstanding example of poverty and isolation in the former communist block. "Did you hear why the Albanian space program has been terminated?" opened one Romanian joke from the 1980s. "Because the last rubber band broke," came the punch line.

* * *

The stories in this book will not be sensational to Albanian readers. They detail the hunger, isolation, and oppression that everyone except the privileged Party members lived with every day in socialist Albania. Through presenting the life stories of normal people in their own narratives, this book is a contribution to the field of Albanian history, which has primarily focused on political history and presented the gendered experiences of men as normative. I have drawn on a wide range of texts to contextualise and verify events. These are cited in footnotes when relevant, and an extensive reference list for further reading is provided at the end of the book.

Between January and July 2010, I recorded more than 200 people talking about their life experiences. When people in shops, cafés, taxis, on public transport, and on the street asked me who I was, my standard reply was that I was an Australian historian writing about the socialist period in Albania. People usually responded that they had lived in that time and could tell me something about it, and I would make myself available to listen for as long as they wanted to talk, either on the spot or at an agreed later time. Many people started talking before I could ask and gain their permission to record, and so I invited them to meet me again and record their words. In line with Australian ethical committee procedures for working with people, I provided information about the project to interviewees, and I recorded their contact details on their signed consent to participate form. Anyone who is cited in this book has been contacted, shown what I have written, and has responded to me. People were free to withdraw their life stories from publication at any time, and I am honoured that numerous people trusted me to write their stories and could then be honest with me and decide not to make those experiences public.

In this work I have aimed to maintain and convey the content that the person cared about, and also to communicate how individuals structured their memories. I want you, the reader, to meet the person as I did, and to exercise your own ability to hear and understand how different people survive and later speak about traumatic experiences. I present the oral history interviews to you in the contexts in which I conducted them, but my own thoughts and analyses of what people have said are clearly delineated as my own, aiming to make my editorial role explicit.

I met Thoma, who is the subject of Chapters One and Two, for half a day every week over six months in 2010, and I continued to meet him at least once a week in the years I have lived in Albania since. Many people spoke for between four and 10 hours of recorded interview time. I lived with a number of families for multiple periods of days. Visits such as these were not recorded, but I conducted specific interviews within the visits to raise subjects I wanted to discuss on the record. I sought out occupational groups through personal networks, such as midwives and military strategy instructors, in order to conduct a quantitatively significant number of interviews. Because I met people while moving through rural and urban Albania on public transport, I interviewed people from all ethnic groups, and women as well as men.

Events in this book are true. Other people or sources have corroborated the occurrence of almost everything recorded in these pages and families of some interviewees read the work in the preparation process. I could verify public events in contemporaneous media sources. I have been careful to record the facts as people remember them, because these personal truths enable us to document and explore the emotional costs and realities of events.

There are, however, three groups of people that barely appear in this book; the Party elite, police and prison guards. Former Politburo and Party elites live without the social marginalisation and fear that characterises the post-socialist lives of those that the Party persecuted,

and they have already written and published their own books justifying
their actions. Many police, *Sigurimi* employees, and former prison guards
were directly recruited to staff local institutions and refusal would have
led to their own persecution; each of these men did their jobs differently.
Their experiences raise questions that require a separate study, but here
we explore the work they did through the experiences of their victims.
This work documents the life experiences of the majority of Albanians,
whose stories have not been told. Included in this category are former
Party secretaries, as each village and co-operative had a committee with
delegates elected from those with good biographies. Through the two
Party secretaries in this book, we witness how collaboration, and the
ways of remembering collaboration, vary between people.

Albanian research assistants were vital to this work. They came to
interviews as cultural chaperones and translators, and transcribed and
translated the recordings afterwards. As Albanian is not my first language,
their presence meant that interviewees didn't need to limit their language,
but they (rightly) assumed that they needed to explain processes and
objects specific to the period in detail to ensure I understood what
they meant. For example, if someone said that they had failed to fulfil
the *norm* and were called to appear before the Party committee, they
would then explain that a *norm* was the expected amount or quota of
daily production, which someone raised in Albania might have been
assumed to know. Interviewees often repeated important statements
and asked if I understood what they were saying to make explicit what
they considered important in their narratives. Being Australian meant
that people trusted there would be no political repercussions (material
or emotional) from speaking with me, which remains a valid concern
in conversations with Albanian journalists or strangers, especially for
formerly politically persecuted women and men.

The research assistants did much more than intellectual
labour – they excelled in the emotional labour required to be engaged
with these histories. They listened to, translated, and transcribed the
repetitions, elisions, and silences of traumatic histories from a world
that their own families had also endured. Edlira Majko, Eriada Çela,

Besiana Lushaj and Sonila Danaj are all established academics and professionals, and I was lucky that they made themselves available for this work. Gjergj Erebara and Luljeta Ikonomi also facilitated multiple interviews and connections, and their knowledge of Albanian history was a great resource and inspiration. You will come to know some of these wonderful people in the pages of this book.

* * *

The structure of this book follows the life stories of six individuals, chosen to provide a broad historical picture of everyday life under communism in Albania for both specialist historians and newcomers to the topic. The three sections unfold key political and social events chronologically, and can be read through for a complete overview of the communist period, or as individual chapters.

In the first section we meet Thoma, a Vlach Albanian born to a shepherding family in 1930, and we follow him through World War Two, Communist Party rule in the 1940s and 1950s, imprisonment in 1966, and his survival after release. We then meet Mevlude Dema, who was born into a family that was politically persecuted. A brilliant chemist, Mevlude worked without professional recognition for her resourcefulness and was exiled from public life, yet she lived a rich intellectual life and made the most unlikely of human connections despite constant surveillance.

The second section tells the stories of two amazing women born to vastly different realities. Both Diana and Liljana studied at university and became teachers in the 1970s, teaching in rural towns in the 1980s. They were not allowed to work in Tirana or close to their families; Diana because her father was arrested for the political crime of agitation and propaganda in 1982, staining her previously good biography, and Liljana because both she and her husband were from ethnic minorities, Egyptian and Romani Albanians.

The third section of the book more closely examines how traumatic events are remembered in present day Albania. A Professor of History, Riza Hasa, grapples with his own history as both a victim and a perpetrator of the regime's cruelties, and we return to the village of his youth to see how the political divide influences life today. In the final chapter, Jeras Naço shares his search for the unmarked grave of his own father, who was executed with fabricated charges of treason and espionage when Jeras was just ten years old. Jeras's quest to find his father's grave takes place in the context of the Albanian post-socialist state's continuing refusal to redress the injustices of the communist period.

Chapter One

Thoma Çaraoshi Joins the Party and Sells the Sheep

In Albania everything happens over coffee. Luljeta introduced me to her father-in-law, Thoma, after I mentioned over coffee that I was interviewing people about life in the communist period. Thoma had recently moved to Tirana to live with his son's family, and we set our first meeting for Monday at 9 a.m. That first Monday, Eda and I walked from our homes in Ali Demi, a suburb at the foothills of Dajti Mountain, to Thoma's neighbourhood behind the city lake, which was land cleared and newly forested with 14-storey apartment blocks. It was my first meeting with Thoma, and Eda's first interview as my research assistant, so we arrived at the designated corner feeling nervous and excited. Luljeta was speaking on her mobile phone. Thoma had not returned home to meet us as planned.

We walked the local streets and enquired at cafés, where baristas told us that Thoma had been spotted drinking his morning espresso, having his hair cut, in conversation with the local dentist, and then strolling in the direction of the city. Back at home Thoma's son reported that he had not returned, so we sat in the café across the road from the house to wait. Luljeta's father waved from the balcony of his nearby flat to show that he understood where to find us. Luljeta was dismayed. Thoma was a stickler for punctuality against the time-bending mainstream of Albanian culture. Perhaps he had forgotten and this was the first sign of old age appearing at the most inconvenient moment? Perhaps something had happened to him?

While we waited, Luljeta reminisced about her childhood in the 1980s, the hungriest years of the communist period. She marvelled that she'd been convinced by the Party's claims that Albania was the richest country on earth. The woman running the otherwise empty café overheard our conversation, introduced herself as Mindie, and joined in with her recollections of life in Kukës, a city in the north, where she lived before the dictatorship fell until 1992. Mindie was the same age as me, but she looked like she'd lived through a lot more. She told us that she was one of eight children from a poor village outside Kukës, and they had picked mountain blueberries in summer to supplement their parents' meagre income from hard agricultural labour. The blueberries were sent for sale in Tirana for medicinal purposes. One of her brothers secured a better-paid job in the mines, dangerous work that left the men chronically ill with back pain and digestive disease. Mindie spoke evenly and fast in a soft voice, as if she had the words long prepared and feared that the moment to share them was too brief. Her mother sat a few tables away, dressed in a traditional long black skirt and apron with a white cotton scarf tied around her head. Mindie told us that her eldest sister had cared for the children at home while her mother worked long hours in the co-operative. One night, the kerosene of the lamp spilt on her sister's body in the bathroom and she was badly burnt. For shame of her nakedness she did not call to the children for help, and she died soon after they found her there the next morning.

While Mindie spoke, her mother lamented a single sentence with increasing volume: "They treated us like dogs in that time!" She pulled herself up with one hand gripping the table and the other her walking stick, and hobbled over to us. She asked my name, rested her stick against the table, and held my face in her hands. She kissed my forehead and focused her blue eyes on my own. "They treated us like dogs," she told me.

Then she turned and shuffled out of the room.

We sat in silence. After a few minutes, the door opened and a tall, well-built man dressed up in a shirt, tie, waistcoat and jacket stepped inside. "Hello! I am Thoma," he boomed, smiling. Mindie jumped back to her waiting position, Eda and I stood to greet Thoma, Luljeta left for work, and Thoma began asking *us* questions. As is usual for first meetings between strangers, especially for older generations of Albanians, Thoma asked Eda what her family name was, where she was born, and where both sides of her family had lived before the demographic movements under the socialist regime. From these questions, complex information about a family's social and political position before, during, and after the socialist period are deduced and applied to individuals. Connections are thus established or broken. Eda's father was from the south, and Eda grew up in the same small city of Delvina where Thoma spent his childhood before World War Two. Thoma declared Eda his cousin, while I fit his category of the single woman far from home. At every meeting he enquired as to the health of my family and whether my apartment in Tirana was warm, and he was gentler with the topic of where to find me a husband than he was with Eda.

We met every week, and Thoma was never again a moment late or confused as to any arrangements. As the weather warmed into spring and then the scorching summer, we met earlier in the mornings, and Thoma led us to cafés further afield, where he was known as a regular patron. Impeccably dressed, and seeming closer to 60 than his 80 years, Thoma proudly introduced us as his "interviewers from Australia" to the wider world of retired men spending time with a coffee, a stiff drink of raki, and their stories. That first meeting had been a ruse of fashionable lateness on his part, effectively heightening the curiosity of the entire neighbourhood as to his whereabouts and the foreigners eager for his presence.

Thoma understands people and it became clear that he enjoyed talking about the past precisely because it troubled him; the ideological contradictions and the question of how he survived could not be easily explained. His stories of finding work and raising a family through waves of political purges were not to be told just once, but perhaps as many times as they had played out in his mind since their occurrence, and Eda and I loved listening. Using language and cultural references grounded in the ethnic diversity of pre-war Southern Albanian society, Thoma's story took us to many worlds and ways of being in these worlds. From his childhood in an ethnic Vlach shepherding family, through the Second World War, and through the decades of communist rule.

*   *   *

Thoma was born in 1932 at his family's home in Delvina, a village separated from the city of Saranda on the Ionian Sea by a single ridge of mountains. Thoma was the third of nine boys and one girl born to his Vlach family, the ethnic minority of shepherds and traders found throughout the Balkans. Vlachs speak Aromanian, which derives from fifteenth-century Romanian language, with more Greek than Slavic-integrated vocabulary. Thoma's grandfather, Mihal Çaraoshi, had migrated to southern Albania with his wife and five children after the First World War. The entire family worked and lived together, and as his grandfather had trained to be an Orthodox priest in Greece, he taught his grandchildren to read and write in Greek language. They spoke Aromanian at home, and attended Albanian primary school in Delvina.

The family tended their flock of sheep and produced dairy products for local villages. In summer they grazed the sheep in the mountains, walking the hills and valleys between Delvina, Gramoz, Skrapar and Mount Tomorr, to the city of Berat. The journey from Delvina to Tomorr took 20 to 30 days – sheep are slow moving animals – and the family slept outside in the *stans*, lean-to, tent-like structures on the hillsides built to protect the sheep from harsh weather, or in inns that catered for shepherds and travellers. The family all worked to milk the sheep twice a day. When the weather was warm, the milk curdled into soft cheese within an hour, and when it was cold they warmed the milk to make the cheese, draining it in cheesecloth hung in the huts along the route and cutting it to sell in the villages and towns they passed on the journey. The cheese sold so quickly that it didn't need to be salted. The family built wooden huts in the mountains where they could leave the cheese-producing equipment safe in winter while they stayed with the flocks in Delvina and Konispol, and the children went to school.

Thoma's father, Mitro, was one of many Albanians who travelled to Italy to modernize his trade in the interwar period. Between 1930 and 1939, Mitro produced cheese with a small American company in Italy, returning every June with his earnings, better production techniques and material culture such as cutlery and glassware to improve the family's living conditions. Mitro invested his earnings in livestock, and by the time that Thoma's grandfather passed away in 1939, the family owned 2000 head of sheep, producing 500 litres of milk and many barrels of cheese per day. Hired shepherds took care of the sheep, and the family lived very well. "Even fish comes to the mountains if you have the money to pay for it," Thoma often said in reference to this time.

Mussolini invaded Albania through the port of Durres on 7 April 1939, and moved south to invade the Kingdom of Greece in October 1940. After the war began, Thoma's father stayed in Delvina with his family and the livestock. Albanian villagers formed partisan groups to fight Italian and then German occupation. The two major partisan groups in the south were the *Balli Kombëtar* (meaning National Front, known as the *Ballists*, formed in October 1939) and the communists from 1941. Both groups hid in the mountains, supported by or stealing from local residents, and villagers of the time didn't necessarily see the *Ballists* and communists as ideological opponents, but rather as both fighting for Albanian independence from foreign occupation. In an early diplomacy lesson, Mitro referred to the sheep stolen by partisans as having been "eaten by war." The sons of the family were thus taught that there were two groups of active partisans in the area, and that men from both sides stole livestock to eat. Mitro was a member of the communist party, and two of his sons fought with them, one losing his life. Thoma, 12 years old at the time, carried messages for partisan units between the villages and towns, escaping suspicion by walking with a donkey laden with wood.

In April 1944, the National Liberation Army (communists) held the Congress of Permet, where an administration was appointed to prepare for post-war Albanian self-government. Thoma and his donkey carried boxes of unknown content to the village of Frasher under the guard of two partisan fighters; he was trusted because his family was known to support the partisan efforts. The communists recognized Vlach families, who had cabins in the highlands, as valuable to the partisan war, and they were treated relatively well by the communist regime until the early 1950s, when their linguistic difference and strong family units were construed as potentially treasonous to Albania. Still, during the war the Çaraoshi family worked to remain on good terms with all Albanian partisans, and they even hid a general of the National Liberation Front in a cave in the mountains after his unit lost a battle. Thoma took him food twice a day for five days until the German offensive withdrew, and this general, who went on to be a powerful Party member in Tirana, proved a vital contact to have when the regime began to persecute the Vlachs and Greeks in the mid-1950s.

Delvina, Italian postcard, Interwar period.

Mount Tomorr viewed from Berat, 2012.

The National Liberation Front claimed to win what they called the War of Liberation in Albania, and they established a provisional government in Berat in October 1944 with Enver Hoxha, a tall and sturdy young partisan from the southern city of Gjirokastër, as prime minister. In the elections of December 1945, the National Liberation Front's successor party, the Democratic Front, won 93% of the vote. Hoxha ruled, primarily by imprisoning and executing all potential rivals, until his death in 1985. In 1945, Enver Hoxha and his partisan peers cut fine figures and presented an agenda that appealed to many young people. They offered an ideologically organized infrastructure for all to participate in a utopian nationalist movement for modernization.

What could be wrong with working together to develop Albania as an independent state, reorganizing production, education and society with a centrally administered plan for the best outcome for all? For the majority of Albanians who owned just small plots of land and who hadn't had the chance to gain an education, the Democratic Front's nationalisation of land and wealth made sense. Those who were politically astute and experienced, and even normal working people who owned property, land, and businesses, quickly understood that they could not avoid the progressive taxation and then seizure of their wealth. Many were branded enemies of the state, as bourgeoisie and kulaks. Enemies were found in every region, even if those punished as kulaks were in fact not much richer than their fellow peasants. Those named enemies were executed or used as imprisoned labour forces. This forced labour completed massive modernization projects such as the draining of the mangroves for arable land in Maliqi and Durres at the cost of many lives, while the Party took the praise for "development" of agriculture and infrastructure. The punishment of kulaks and their families was an example to others of what lay on the opposite side of enthusiastic support for the party, and these constantly "unmasked" enemies provided a shifting focus to maintain anxiety amongst the people.

Thoma's father Mitro noted the communists' overarching discourse of revolution by arms and without dissent, and he remained a member of the Democratic Front. He did not ask for compensation for the livestock "eaten by the war," and he explained to his sons that there was a difference between consistent moral law (as in the Bible and the Koran) and the harsh laws of ever-changing rulers. As Thoma still says to explain post-socialist politics, "If you break the law of the state, the law groans, and its owner seeks to punish those who have caused it to weep." In recounting stories from throughout his life, Thoma would often use this metaphor to make meaning of the arbitrary nature of the law, and the cruelties of those who acted and still act in its name.

The teenage Thoma, however, saw the triumphant, young, and strong men of the communist movement as harbingers of a luminous future, and it was only through the trials of the next twenty years that he came to understand his father's wisdom and see political power as an arbitrary and shifting force. At the end of the war, Thoma saw Enver Hoxha, who marched into Tirana with his armed comrades, as "the new king," and he decided to stand with them. Considering his intelligence, energy, and his family's good standing with the Party, in 1951 Thoma was admitted to military school in Tirana for a year of ideological and tactical studies. Thoma travelled to Tirana with the energy and hope of a young man who saw the way to help rebuild Albania.

Enver Hoxha emphasised the vital role of youth to lead the country to its glorious destiny, and he blamed the poverty of agrarian society on the ruling classes, the monarchy, and previous bourgeois governments. The Democratic Front promised education, employment and remuneration to all, and relied on full social participation to staff the schools, agricultural co-operatives, and factories that would industrialize Albania. In the late 1940s and throughout the economic developments of the 1950s, Enver Hoxha presented the socialist movement as a collective where youth bound by the blood losses of war could sacrifice personal interest for national development. The power of a shared goal to make Albania strong equalized and mobilized the post-war youth, and they learnt about socialism in ideological classes and through propaganda. While Thoma was from a beautiful part of the country abundant in food, other youth recruits in his classes shared their experiences of harsh living conditions and poverty, and Thoma understood the appeal of the promised life of plenty to those who were raised in poverty.

Thoma remembers that heady atmosphere – there was shared work, food, and travel for the groups of young, energetic men. The Albanian-Soviet alliance provided the possibility to travel to Moscow for education, and reassured all that independent Albania now had powerful and vast allies to defend the national borders from attacks such as those of the Italian and German occupations in World War Two. Thoma aimed to build socialism, join the Party and travel to Moscow for a diplomatic education. As his father had travelled to Italy before the war to support their family, he also planned to pursue opportunities abroad. Socialism made sense to Thoma. It was an honourable extension of his family's ethic of hard work, meritocracy, and the inalienable bond of family to include the national Albanian family in which all could work and prosper.

After graduation in 1952, Thoma was sent to work as a Party Youth Secretary with the Fifth Division in Hoxha's hometown of Gjirocastër in Southern Albania. This was a bureaucratic and ideological position, not a military position, and Commissars (political instructors in the Soviet style) taught that when socialist society developed into communism, there would be just two hours of work a day and a lot to eat. Many young men in the military were hungry from the constant physical construction work and many, like Thoma, missed the bounty of pre-war home life. Once, the 18-year-old Thoma asked a Commissar when he estimated that communism would be achieved, and the Commissar replied "When our eyes pop out. When we're dead. Never. But keep your mouth shut!" Thoma was shocked and perplexed. He'd read Marx and Lenin, he liked Hoxha's vision of a modernized and independent Albania. He blamed the laziness of his increasingly demoralized comrades for the shortcomings and whispered criticisms of the new government. It was at this point that Thoma became aware of the gap between ideology and practice.

In 1952, Thoma was accepted as a member of the Communist Party and he worked in the southern city of Gjirokastër, supervising work units. By this time, as secret intelligence reports attest, the flagging morale of soldiers and the lack of ideological commitment of police and officers had become an issue of concern for the upper echelons of the military.[1] One day in 1953, the general that Thoma had saved in the war visited Gjirokastër as a high ranking official inspector. He recognized Thoma at work before Thoma could place him. "You brought me bread with cheese, don't you remember?" he reminded Thoma, and then asked him whether he missed his family. With the fearlessness of inexperience, Thoma told him that all the soldiers wanted to go home so they could eat well. He refused the general's offer of money, telling him that his father never left his sons without money. The general then gave him 20 days leave and Thoma visited his family. Each time he recounted this story to Eda and I, Thoma added that he searched for the general again when his brother was imprisoned in 1965, without success. Thoma next met the general in 1966, in his own prison cell.

Thoma tired of the gap between the theory of what was possible for Albanian development and the facts on the ground.

> We were poor because we weren't working. I was a Brigadier and a Party Secretary. I had three girls, four women and 20 men working in my brigade. They worked only three hours and then hid. Enver told them to work for their salary but they complained – they didn't want to work and they wanted the money. I wrote a letter to the Party Committee saying that revisionism had attacked my brigade. "They are revisionists, they don't work and they want money," I wrote. Then the Party came and asked me if I wrote the letter. I told them yes, because I cannot supervise people if they hide when they are supposed to work. They told me to keep my mouth shut.

The next day Thoma told the director that he couldn't work there anymore, and that he would leave the military a year earlier than he was

1   6 March 1952 report of Hamit Matjani to Albanian royalist headquarters in Rome in Owen Pearson, *Albania in the Twentieth Century A History Vol. 3 1946-1990* (London: I. B. Tauris, 2007), 441.

supposed to rather than dishonour himself with lies in the workplace. He also wanted to return to live in Berat with his new wife.

At age 21, Thoma married Maria, a 19-year-old woman from another Vlach family. It was an arrangement between their fathers which had been promised in their youth, in the tradition of bringing good families together through marriage. Hoxha later forbade child betrothals during the Cultural and Ideological Revolution of 1967, but in the 1950s Vlach families were still organized by the patriarchs and their wives. Despite the Party's attempts to weaken and replace the role of traditional family structures, patriarchal control of the family remained strong. There was, however, already disagreement in Thoma's family about whether to hold a church wedding (in line with Orthodox religion and tradition) or to refuse any religious ceremony as antithetical to Party ideology. Thoma's fiancée and mother demanded the church wedding despite Thoma's commitment to communist atheism, and they later baptized all the children in secret, undeterred by the Party's execution of clergy found conducting these rituals.

Thoma provided the best of both modern and traditional wedding ceremonies:

> We celebrated weddings like this: we decided the date when we would go to take the bride. One week before that we put up the three flags of the wedding, one was rose colour, for the bride, white was for the groom, and one was red, the national colour. We traditionally took the bride from her family's home on horseback. We Orthodox used to take two women along with us because it was a long way, three or four hours by horse, and she might have needed some help from other women.
>
> Three of us went when I took my wife, and I took my bride with a car, not a horse. I took my wife with the car because I had a friend in Tirana who had a good position and he lent me a brand new brown car. I went with my two brothers and my sister to my wife's family in Kolonja, ate and slept there, and the next day we took the bride and drove to Elbasan, Berat, and to Tomorr Mountain

where my family were. We celebrated until Monday morning, and at midday on Monday we married in church. My wife was young, only 19 years old, and to travel there by horse would have been tiresome for her. We climbed Tomorr Mountain with the mules. We had music, meat on the spit, *byrek*, and a lot of things: a feast. Enver made it a little bit difficult to do all these things, but we were still rich at that time so we could find food to buy.

My family lived on the mountain, and on our wedding night I brought my wife home to a room that was full of barrels of fresh feta cheese and *gjizë*. Right up until she passed away she reminded me of that moment and scolded me, "How could you take me to that room that stank of cheese for the first night of our marriage!"

In 1955 the formation of co-operatives on arable land was made mandatory by law. The Politburo decided how Albanian land, agriculture and livestock should be handled, while the USSR pushed for Albania to grow citrus for export in return for Soviet grain. The Albanian government pursued agricultural and industrial production for self-sufficiency in grain and all other goods, seeing itself as isolated amidst hostile neighbours. Ties with Yugoslavia to the north were cut in 1947, and there was an on-going declared state of war with Greece to the south. Due to the lack of suitable arable land and the post-war population boom, Albania never achieved self-sufficiency in grain production. In fact, production fell over the four decades of self-sufficiency policy. The state acquisition of private land and goods happened in a haphazard way, primarily influenced by the location and value of the commodity, who wanted it, and how easy it was to take. The first co-operatives were thus formed on the most arable land, and the private houses of former land owners, non-communist intellectuals, and statesmen were seized to be used as state buildings or homes for the new Party elite.

The tightly knit Vlach community across Southern Albania relied on travelling across regions to graze their flocks and sell dairy products, so they kept a close eye on what was happening. They had a higher level of access to information than others due to their mobility for business and trade networks, and many Vlachs decided to escape Albania or to sell their produce and settle in the cities before they were forced to relinquish their stock to the co-operatives. Numerous memoirs and international reports of escapes across the southern border to Greece after 1950 were published and presented to the United Nations.[2] When escape attempts failed, people were imprisoned in the extensive system of forced labour camps for political opponents of the new regime. Many were tortured, and some attempted escape again. The border was heavily policed, and the declared state of war between Greece and Albania in October 1940 was not lifted until 1987, although diplomatic relations resumed in 1971.

Having heard and read many accounts of how difficult it was to cross the border alive, Eda and I were shocked when Thoma told us that in 1956 his cousin, Foto Basha, walked across the Greek border with not only his flock of 1000 sheep, but also 57 members of his family. Indeed, *The Times* reported this event on September 11, 1956.

> 60 Albanian nomads, leading 1000 sheep, crossed the Greek frontier over the week-end and asked for asylum from the Greek authorities. They claimed that they had "neutralized" the frontier guards at the Albanian outpost. The nomads were given permission to camp outside the border town of Konicë.[3]

Foto Basha had been a communist partisan in the war, and was a general in the army and a Party member, so the Party had trusted him to graze his sheep near the border outside Korça. Three days before he fled, Foto had met Thoma for a coffee and told him of his plan. The family had

2 See the unpublished report by a group of Albanians who escaped, calling themselves the National Committee for a Free Albania, "Testimony on Slave Labour Conditions within Albania," submitted to the United Nations and the US Government in 1952, used in the compilation of the US Government's 1955 submission to the UN entitled "Evidence of the Existence of Forced Labour in Albania." Held in the Library of Congress, USA.

3 *The Times*, September 11 1956. Cited in Pearson, *Albania in the Twentieth Century*, 511.

realized it would look suspicious if they all travelled to Korça to escape together, so they had not joined him. Foto alone had taken the sheep from the co-operative as usual, met his family in the fields near the border, and calmly and quickly crossed with his family, hidden on their hands and knees amongst the sheep.

When Thoma told this story I was amazed. I laughed out loud at the daring simplicity of the escape, but Thoma just shook his head.

> His name was all over the newspapers. When he went to Greece, he talked to the radio and TV about the situation in Albania, that the government here had taken our animals and land. He knew that we would end up in prison but he didn't care. He knew what he wanted, I bear him no grudge. Everybody can choose a better place to live. I knew that people lived better abroad. I used to listen to the radio at night.

As he expected, the state came for him the very next day. Thoma was taken to the police station and interrogated. His strategy was to criticize his cousin's defection in the interrogation and to offer to do so in Party meetings also. Thoma considered himself lucky to have avoided imprisonment or worse. "They could have asked me to follow him and kill him, but I don't think I could have returned alive, because my cousin was very brave. But they didn't ask me."

Requests for family members to participate in revenge against traitors were not uncommon – the regime worked hard to make the Party the centre of power and control rather than the patriarchs of extended family networks. When I asked Thoma if he really thought that following Foto Basha to kill him would have been an option, he looked at me and said in an uncharacteristically tired and quiet voice, "Shannon, you need to understand one thing. That government was like God; it could kill you and you couldn't say anything against it."

* * *

In an attempt to transfer capital before it was confiscated by the state, between 1956 and 1958 Thoma sold the family's donkeys and traded in hand-made saws, saving the significant sum of two million lek. In 1958, the family sold half the flock to the co-operative and bought a 14-bedroom house in Elbasan, large enough for all nine brothers and their wives. It was the tradition for men to bring their wives into the family home. Thoma remembers this period as a time of continuing affluence for them. Neither Maria nor Thoma's brothers' wives worked, and Thoma worked as a Party manager of exports in Durres, supervising the export of Albanian meat and cheese to Romania, Czechoslovakia, Bulgaria, and Greece. Hundreds of thousands of lambs were exported to Greece for Easter, despite the political non-engagement between the states. This international trade was possible because of the boom in agricultural production due to nationalised co-operatives staffed with total labour mobilization and new lands made available by the forced labour of political prisoners. Money was not a problem for the Çaraoshi family, and Thoma's father and mother closely managed the families of their nine sons.

Politically persecuted workers, including the writer Kasëm Trebeshina, were amongst those Thoma worked with in Durres. He recalled taking other workers to a hotel in Durres on Saturday nights to give Trebeshina privacy with his wife on her weekly visits. As Eda and I met Thoma through the months, Thoma said that memories came to him at night, and that he had remembered something Trebeshina had told him, "You need to write when the thoughts come, in the dark."

* * *

As a Party Secretary in Elbasan in the early 1960s, Thoma had very little work to do in order to earn the salary of 11,000 lek per month. He had to attend monthly communist committee meetings, and he explained his changing relationship to the Party by saying it was like a couple that marry, have children, and then want to get divorced five years later, when it is no longer possible to divorce without serious repercussions for the entire family. "Nobody forced me to join the Party," Thoma explained, "but once I was in and saw how it was, it was too late to get out of it."

One task of the monthly Party meetings in Elbasan was to judge applications for divorce. In the Cultural and Ideological Revolution of the 1960s, the Party openly assumed the role of moral and social arbiter of all aspects of life, especially involving themselves in the family as the primary social institution. Some women brought their complaints of being beaten or neglected by their husbands before the Party and requested divorce. Under the 1955 legal code, which claimed to modernize "archaic and patriarchal feudo-bourgeois family laws," divorce could be granted only with a blame clause against one party. Thoma and the committee attempted to reconcile marriages rather than allow them to pass further to the court system, as Party bureaucrats close to the ground in the early 1960s felt more comfortable placing "personal" problems back in the hands of immediate family networks. Party members were also afraid of being accused of breaking up families if they allowed divorces to go through, so the predominantly male committees advised women to appease their husbands in order to avoid domestic violence. This was also in line with the traditional patriarchal values of society.

The Party meetings dealt with all kinds of issues: relationships between people, economic planning, employment issues, crimes of all kinds, ideological education, and denunciations. At each meeting, the committee first heard about crimes. All notes taken from every meeting were forwarded to the Central Committee, and crimes of property theft worth more than 2,000 lek as well as other serious criminal acts were forwarded to the prosecutor.

The atmosphere was always tense. Thoma described Committee meetings as "war." Anyone could stand up and denounce someone for stealing, or for saying something that may have been true but could not be said, such as questioning the inflated numbers of the annual agricultural production, or asking why there was no food in the market while so much was packaged for export. When one Party member denounced another, the accused had to defend themselves. When I asked Thoma if it was better to remain quiet or to fight an accusation, he replied that anyone who falls in the sea should try to save themselves, and if they don't succeed they will drown, but if they don't try, they will drown anyway.

The most persistent problem for the Committee at this time was the theft of food and basic items by women with families to feed. Sometimes the committee recommended a person to be moved to another position, usually to physical labour in the collective farm, as a demotion. A worker accused of laziness would be moved to work with someone with a good reputation and ordered to work as a unit and divide the salary between them. This imposed a variety of social pressures to correct and control both overactive and underactive labour, in reality forcing hard workers to carry the burden. Public shaming was a common punishment.

Thoma gave the example of somebody stealing something small, such as a glass, and being brought before the gathered members of the collective and berated. The leader would point at the accused and yell. "You stole! Villain, that belongs to the state! We have so many workers, if everybody stole the factory would all be stolen." When a sheep was stolen, the skin was peeled off the animal and wrapped around the shoulders of the accused thief, who had to walk through the market so that everyone could see and they were shamed. Thefts considered abnormal, in that they were without motive or were of items worth more than 2000 lek (about half a standard monthly salary), were punished as espionage and carried prison terms.

Thoma told us that Hoxha himself said, "the collective is the strongest court," but he often felt and sometimes voiced his discomfort with the Committee members' confidence in judging people accused and denounced before them. "Did Jesus steal?" Thoma would ask Eda and I. "No! That is because Jesus didn't have a family to feed! Show me someone with children who doesn't try to feed them." On one occasion a man was accused of stealing some pieces of wood from the collective, and Thoma knew, as everyone did, that there were none amongst them who had not taken small amounts of food or materials from the state. As the criticism of the man continued, Thoma stood up and said, "How can I judge this man as if I am the court? What judge am I? I don't have school! A lawyer studies law! I don't know any articles of law with which to judge the theft of a piece of wood!" The other committee members shouted at him to sit down and accused him of being friends with the thief. The system relied on the fact that everyone was poor enough to be driven to steal. As long as everyone could be accused of stealing, those who stole the most were the ones who vocally denounced others in order to pre-emptively protect themselves from denunciation. Thoma often said that hungry dogs bark the loudest, and it was well known that the state paid witnesses in cash or in favours. The hungriest people were most often present as witnesses in trials.

* * *

In 1961, Albania sided with China in the Sino-Soviet split, and in 1964 the Albanian Communist Party broke with the USSR under Kruschev's leadership. The USSR had provided political, financial and industrial support to Albania, and Albanians had seen the USSR as protection against hostility from Yugoslavia, Greece and capitalist foes further afield. Students and workers travelled to the USSR for education, and the Russians were lauded on visits to Albania.

Albanians perceived their new ally, China, as radically different in culture to Europe, and many Albanians acutely felt the loss of the alliance with the USSR. This was the beginning of Hoxha's progressive isolationism. The split shocked Thoma. On the day that the announcement was made, he was supervising 83 workers in Elbasan market as Party Secretary, when the Party called a meeting for all 17 Party Secretaries from Elbasan district. A woman he worked with was married to the Chief of Police, and she whispered to him that the meeting was called because Hoxha had broken with the Russians. Thoma replied, "How could this be true?"

"Don't say anything or you will be charged with treason. Just say 'We don't know the Russians, we are with Enver; long live Enver Hoxha,'" she warned him.

After the break with Russia, productivity quotas (called the *norm*) increased, salaries decreased, and the number of secret police, the

Sigurimi, increased. In his own version of Mao Zedong's Cultural Revolution, Enver Hoxha initiated a purge of anyone with a strong connection to the USSR, bureaucrats, technocrats, religion, and the youth. The 1964 constitution evidenced the turn to paranoid isolationism as the ideological basis for Party actions, exemplified in the most common slogan: *VIGILENCE.* Anyone who was associated with escape attempts or with enemies of the state could expect a prison sentence, and waves of trials for association and fabricated accusations of treason took place in every city throughout the mid to late 1960s. The legal injunction against contact with enemies of the state was intended to break the trust within extended families, especially those of Greek and Vlach ethnic origin, on the grounds of their supposed connections to foreign governments. The strengths of Vlach families like Thoma's, multilingualism and family solidarity, thus became likely reasons for political persecution.

In 1964, one of Thoma's brothers who had fought with the Communist Partisans in the war and was thus held in esteem by the Party, was arrested and sent to prison. Thoma's brother had brought his elderly godmother, the mother of Foto Basha (who had escaped eight years earlier) to live in his home. The imprisonment of one brother was the Party's strike at the entire traditional family.

> The system was like this: in each good family one was sent to prison. We could live well, even though he was in prison. We worked, but we no longer had the shine as a family that we'd had before. We went to visit our brother every Saturday. At that time, the parents, siblings, wife, and children of a prisoner could visit. We weren't afraid to visit because he was family – everyone knew we would support him, as he had supported his godmother. If anyone else went to visit him they had to write down their names and they were asked why they went there and would be under surveillance from that moment. My father said this about communism: "everything that is born will die." We were attacked after my brother was sent to prison, even though another brother had died in the war. Now that I remember, just now, I'm shivering.

But my father told us not to be upset, as everything that is born will die – that he might die but we would live to see it. And he was right – all of my siblings lived to see communism fall.

Thoma was removed from the Party and thus lost his job, but because of his good friends in high Party places, he was sent to work in the market as a trader, not to agricultural work. Other members of his family, however, were sent to work as labourers. Despite the communist system claiming 100% employment, the state actually refused to assign people to work as a form of persecution in itself. Thoma's wife was not given a place to work for three years, in which time she was required to present herself at the Party employment office and ask for a work assignation every day, only to be sent home again.

In this time, Thoma began to secretly build sofas at home at night with his wife and two daughters in order to earn extra money. Because he had been raised in an entrepreneurial extended family, and had strong established social networks throughout Elbasan, they made money although they worked in fear of being caught. As the persecution of the family intensified, limiting his children's education and employment chances, black market work kept the family afloat and enabled Thoma to save in case he himself was sent to prison for any length of time.

In our interviews Thoma told a few of his stories often, turning a desperate undertaking with little chance of success into a David and Goliath story of good versus evil. One of Thoma's favourite stories was about the time he went to see Enver Hoxha in 1965.

I decided that no one could solve my problem but Enver, not Mehmet [Mehmet Shehu, Premier of Albania at the time], only Enver. I wanted to meet Enver, he was like a king to us! And the second reason I wanted to meet him was that he could solve my problem. I was really excited to go to meet him! I have had money all my life, and loyal friends. I went to his office. I knew where it was, and they directed me to go to one room. I knocked at the door and somebody said "Come in," but when I entered the room a woman around 40 years old was there!

Listen, I had a very beautiful wife, so other women were nothing to me. This was my fate. Anyway, when I saw that this was a woman I turned around to leave. I said, "Sorry, I knocked at the wrong door, I am here to meet Enver." She told me that she was Enver! I told her, "Excuse me, you cannot be Enver because he is a man!" I had a discussion with her about this and in the end she accepted that she was not Enver, but that Enver told her to meet me, but I told her that what I wanted to say to Enver I could not tell her. She became angry and told me that they would take measures against me for saying that, but I responded with bad words I can't repeat to you, and I left.

The office notified Elbasan and the Party Secretary called me into his office and asked me if I had been in Tirana. I said yes and he asked me why. I responded that I had wanted to meet Enver. I was still a communist at that time, but they almost imprisoned me. I had a friend in the Party who told me that he often met Enver and he told me to write him a letter and to tell him when I posted it. This friend told me that letters addressed to Enver weren't read by him, but by his secretaries, but my friend helped me so that the letter could arrive in Enver's hand. Enver replied with a letter to the Party in Elbasan. He wrote that if the citizen (which was me) was lying then he was to be arrested, but that if the Party Secretary was lying then he was to be arrested. They sent secret agents to the queues to see what was happening. They saw that the Secretary really was removing people that he didn't like from the food queues. He was only rebuked for his behaviour but not arrested. However, he got scared of what could happen to him and he died just six months later. You see! You can have a good heart, but what matters is what your tongue says. The tongue doesn't have bones, but it can break bones!

This story is a bit confusing. The first few times I heard Thoma tell this story I was stunned by his respect for Hoxha, whom he refers to by his first name as if they were friends, and whom Thoma trusted to make fair decisions for "the people." In Thoma's story, the "King" is thwarted by evil-doers (female secretaries and Party bureaucracy), and his story asserts his economic self-sufficiency, social networking skills and luck in finding a beautiful wife. Thoma's quest to meet the King is the objective of the story at the start, and yet the story ends with the wrong-doer identified and dying with shame at having been uncovered, rendering revenge unnecessary. The moral of the story is, ostensibly, that the tongue has more power to implement justice than good will without voice.

It was only after I'd become familiar with this story that I figured out what information was missing. "What was the problem that you took to Enver Hoxha?" I asked him. Thoma's reply was confusing and fragmented, he didn't like to tell the story directly. I pieced it together to understand exactly what had happened. A local Party deputy had been removing his wife from the daily queues for food and refused to give her a work position. This persecution and enforced unemployment in the socialist system meant that she was not able to bring home food for the children and led Thoma to undertake what was in fact a risky move that required a great deal of bravado in the face of a hostile bureaucracy and a potentially hostile Enver Hoxha. Thoma's courage in demanding justice from the centre of power is the underlying heroism of the story, a traumatic interaction re-presented as a confidence to demand the worker's state protect the right of people to work. Thoma's story of meeting Enver Hoxha is celebratory and elides the difficult context of persecution because it belongs to the brief time when Thoma could claim to be worthy of respect from the socialists; he still believed that the persecution of his entire family for his brother's relationship with his godmother was wrong and the result of individuals thwarting Party policy. This all changed with his arrest and imprisonment in 1966.

Chapter Two

Life is War

I would always ask Thoma after about three hours together whether he was becoming tired. Thoma would dismiss the very notion. "Tired?" he'd exclaim, throwing his shoulders back and reaching out his arms, expressing indignation and surprise. "When I was in prison I had three interrogators, THREE!" It was unsettling to be reassured by a favourable comparison with police interrogation. Thoma always took my concern as the opening for him to recount the events of his arrest and imprisonment in 1966, with increasing detail each week. When Thoma raised the spectre of his time in prison he hurried his speech, rushing through a non-chronological sequence of oft-repeated anecdotes revolving around the hunger, the beatings and the psychological torture. My methodology as an oral historian was to let Thoma, as with everyone I interviewed, speak without interruption for as long or as little time as he wanted. These repeated pockets of seemingly confused attempts to explain a specific event or period are the markers of trauma: episodes that remain unable to be integrated in one's dominant sense of social self, even decades after they have occurred.

Each week I listened and gradually pieced the new and old parts of

his story together in chronological order, and the complete account is
as follows:

When they came and arrested me at home they told me that I
was just being taken for work somewhere, but as soon as they
put me in the car they tied my hands together. I started to laugh.
I understood what was happening. "Why are you laughing?" One
of them asked me, and I said I was laughing because I was arrested
because of who my brothers were. "You're not the first to say that,"
one of them answered.

They took me to the police station. I had a pair of shoes that cost
3,500 lek, the monthly salary of a worker. A general-major saw
my good shoes and insulted me with the old saying about women
sent to live with their husbands: "Ah, bride, where you put your
feet, you will lose also your teeth" [*Nuse, ku vure këmbët, do të
humbësh dhëmbët*]. I asked him if he was Lab, one of those from
the region of southern Albania renowned as fighters, and he said
he was. I told him that we Vlachs simply say *Inshallah*, as God
wishes. "Oooah!" he said. "We were told that you were a party
member and now you also believe in God?"

"Even Enver Hoxha believes in God. When Enver goes home in
the evening he says, 'Thank God I am alive!'" I replied.

They took everything from me, all my buttons, money. I had
42,000 lek with me, the annual salary of an interrogator. At home
I had hidden enough money to support my family for five years,
in case I was imprisoned. I was hard-working.

"Why have you arrested me?" I asked them.

"For political reasons."

"What have I done? I joined the Party in 1951."

"In which group?"

They implied that I was associated with a group of traitors purged
since that time.

"I joined the Party of Labor," I replied.

"Do you accept these interrogators?"

I said I accepted only if they were Albanians and I laughed, because they were accusing me of being against Albania! How could Albanians fight me?

The one that arrested me left and the interrogators took me. I stayed 99 days in a cell. Then they gave me back everything, even the money, and I was released because I was innocent.

For those 99 days I had three interrogators: one Lab, one from Korça on the Greek border, and one from Shkodra in the North. The one from Korça beat me. One of the others told him not to hit me, as I might die and leave the children orphans. They didn't leave me alone. They stayed 24 hours in eight-hour shifts: eight hours one, eight hours the others. They made a circle on the floor and asked me to stand there without moving for eight hours. But could you stay eight hours standing? If I moved – POW! They would hit me. I hope you never go there. The only food they gave me was one potato in the evening. Every Sunday my wife brought me clothes and food – meat, baklava – but I didn't receive anything. The policemen ate it. I got only a potato. They brought water once a day or every two days, so as not to dehydrate me. They would drink in front of me. When I went to prison I weighed 75 kg, and I came out weighing only 47 kg.

The cell was so small that when I stood, the ceiling was one hand higher than my head. There was a small window for fresh air and a house behind the prison wall. I could hear the music and the children. There was a small window in the door to pass cigarettes through, but they didn't bring me anything because I was arrested for political reasons. Political prisoners were more harshly treated than simple criminals. My wife couldn't see me. The interrogators told me that my mother had died, but in fact she was still alive. I reassured myself that my thoughts were not secure – they were playing with my mind, and I knew not to let myself consider anything they said as truth. The interrogators were saying things so that I would talk, but I was stubborn because I had not done anything.

One day, the Chief came with a man from Tirana and asked me two
questions. I knew this man – he was the very good friend of mine
from the war, the one whom I had hidden and fed when he was
injured. I had looked for him when my brother was imprisoned
because in those times you could work to fix things with friends,
but I couldn't find him then. He came from Tirana dressed in
white clothes, looking important. I told him that I hadn't done
anything. He couldn't stand upright in the cell because his head
touched the ceiling. He came there without the interrogators,
accompanied by the Chief of Police, who told him that I was not
obeying the guards. He told me that he was a general and I said,
"I don't know who you are." I gained points there, I didn't betray
our relationship. He told me that he came directly from Tirana
when he heard that they had arrested me. He told me that I had
to say a word. For 95 days I hadn't said yes to their accusations,
only no. He asked me again, "Yes or no?" I said no. He asked me
again. The Chief of Police was smoking.

Suddenly I was down. I was pushed to the ground. "Yes or no?"
I again said no. He asked me how they were treating me in the
interrogation. I said that they threatened to send me to prison if
I continued to refute their accusations. He asked me for the last
time, yes or no. I said no. He said ok and good day, and left. They
didn't even give me a cigarette.

Three days later Thoma was released.

My friend from Tirana told them to release me. In the morning
the interrogator from Korça told the Police Chief to let me go
home because I had family and I had a brother in prison. He felt
sorry for me. I wished the Chief a long life to his wife and the
Party. But once when he was beating me I had said, "I will be
released and I hope you get cancer, so I can see your soul come
out of your arse." At the time, he beat me harder. But you know,
he later suffered from cancer. I met him once on the street and

I asked him why he was so thin. He told me he was sick. I said
that maybe it is the cancer, just as I had cursed him. He died.
They have all died, but I am still alive. They didn't punish you for
nothing. If you don't eat garlic, you don't smell; my family had
broken the law according to their laws – we helped each other
within the family. But I suffered for 99 days. When I went home
I could hardly walk. Life is war.

On the day Thoma was released from prison, his wife had again gone
to ask the Head of the People's Council for work. There was money at
home, but Maria was tired of *Sigurimi* officers following her everywhere,
and since she was the head of the family while Thoma was in prison, she
wanted to work. He said there were no jobs for women, even though so
many factories had just opened. She knew this man because he had come
to their house when Thoma was Party Secretary. He had been watching
Thoma because the Party Secretary could communicate directly with
the central committee while the municipal head could not. Yet in his
office he had asked her whose wife she was, and when she answered
Thoma Çaraoshi he had shouted at her to leave and she had hurried
home crying. When Thoma knocked on the door, Maria feared it was
the police coming to arrest her also, and called out, "Who's there?"

"It's me!" I replied, and she opened the door, and then they all
hugged me. My beard was so long, my fingernails were long.
I was filthy. Nobody asked me about where I had been when I came
out of prison. They were afraid. Only my wife, brothers, mother
asked, but I said nothing, even to them. My mother cried and
asked me if I had eaten in prison. "Of course I did," I told her. "But
then why are you so thin?" She cried. When I met someone else,
even if I knew he had been persecuted or in prison, we couldn't
speak. After my time in prison I saw the regime differently: I was
afraid. The government is like God, it can kill you and you can't
say anything against it.

We could say that Thoma's time in prison destroyed the last shreds of his hope for a socialist society, but due to his character and the strength of his family, it was also the moment when he came to understand the power of his enemies in the system, outside of his formerly cherished ideology. He had challenged the state on the egalitarian grounds of communist ideology and realized that the language of class liberation simply masked individual struggles for power, as they had before the war. The dictatorship of the proletariat was not the proletariat rule he had worked for in his youth, it was the dictatorship of those in power over those who worked, and now the dictatorship's gaze was fixed on his family, including his young children.

Thoma was expelled from the Party. He was deposed from his secure and high-ranking workplace to spend more than twenty years working in a rotation of jobs, constantly aware of being under *Sigurimi* surveillance as a tainted ex-Party member. Thoma's life was dominated by the struggle to support his family in the controlled socialist system, trying to protect them from further political persecution through unpredictable waves of purges at all levels, as well as pervasive poverty. I asked Thoma whether he had complained about the guards who beat him or the *Sigurimi* who followed him after the fall of the regime. He answered that he didn't because he understood what they had done; they had been told to do it. "But could you do the job of a prison guard? Or an informer?" I asked him. "No. Those people were black-hearted. The state relied on them. This is a subject that could fill a thousand novels."

Thoma always stressed the importance of work. He would share his latest ideas for making small businesses with Eda and I, and laugh about the jobs he had made for himself in the 1990s, when he became free to work how and where he wanted. Thoma often told Eda and myself two specific anecdotes about work. One was that there is a reason that all Christians make the sign of the cross. You touch your shoulders first because the arms need to work for a living, then the head, which needs to think carefully about how to work, and finally the stomach, which needs to be filled regardless of politics or personal preferences. Thoma would also say, "The state is like a body; at the heart is the Party – it controls everything in the system. The arms and legs do the hard work that the heart controls. And the blood? The blood is the *Sigurimi*."

This was Thoma's understanding of the system he had survived, and his place in it. In order to eat and live, one had to think and work in line with the party to avoid the punishment of the pervasive secret police. Thoma explained, "The law groans when it is hurt, and the owner of the law will find you and punish you." In Thoma's reflections on the decades he lived as an unwilling and untrusted former Party member, he refers to the "nervous problems" he and his family suffered, what I would diagnose as intense stress and resultant depression, through which he had to work long hours and monitor everything he thought and said.

Between 1964 and 1974, the Politburo directed waves of purges against Vlach and Greek minority communities. Enver Hoxha presented his split with the Soviet Union as an anti-Imperialist strike for Albanian national independence, directing shock waves of intensified paranoia and political persecution toward Albanian citizens with possible international links. Russian women who had married Albanian men and moved to Albania were imprisoned, their husbands forced to renounce the marriages or be imprisoned themselves. Throughout the 1960s, Elbasan in particular was the site of continual "unmaskings" of supposed traitors against Albania, due to its location at the centre of the fertile agricultural region with significant minority communities. Many innocent ethnic minority Albanians were arrested and publicly tried on fabricated charges of espionage and Greek-sponsored terrorism in the Elbasan court and then executed in secret locations. Thoma was in Elbasan throughout the arrest, public trial and execution of Apostol Naço (Chapter Eight in this book), for example, and there were other show trials, imprisonments, and executions that successfully isolated everyday people in a terrifying awareness that anything could happen to them at any time. Thoma and his brothers broke with family tradition and sent their wives to work in the community. Everyone in the Vlach and Greek minority communities understood the vital importance of never speaking any minority language in public or showing any relationships with other members of the community beyond the standard working relationships. In this way, the centrally directed and fabricated so-called "anti-Imperialist" purges in the 1960s isolated individuals in fear for their lives, and paved the way for the state of paranoid militarized isolation that was total by the time that Hoxha broke the Sino-Albanian alliance in 1978.

After prison, Thoma was moved from workplace to workplace 15 times. First he was removed from his job in the export company and sent to work in the marketplace, where he could be closely watched and easily accused of treason. As a salesperson in the market for four years, he was careful that his books and the inventory always balanced so that the Party could not accuse him of anything. He also maintained social networks of support. Even though you could not change the state-controlled prices of goods, and even though the queues for the products in season were long, he sometimes gave credit using his own money as a balance until customers could pay. Prices for all items were set by the State in relation to wages in order to ensure there would be no inflation or surplus income which could lead people to be frustrated by the lack of consumable items, including food. Thoma earnt 7,500 Lek per month in this job, which was less than a Party functionary but more than a labourer.

The next position Thoma was moved to was collecting and valuing old furniture from people's homes, providing them with a receipt for state compensation for the value of the item, then taking it and fixing it up as new for poorer people to buy. They would buy a chair for 100 lek, for example, and sell it for 200 lek, and he was paid per piece that he salvaged. In this job Thoma had to visit the notorious psychiatric hospital in Elbasan, a hospital prison. The state at the time argued that this hospital provided free psychiatric care, but it was really a prison for political detainees. Those detained by force in the psychiatric hospital were mostly young and middle-aged people, including university lecturers and the teenage children of Albanians who had returned from Australia and America to be immediately imprisoned. The imprisoned patients were not only those who spoke against the system, but also regular female and male prisoners moved and held there to keep them separate from the prison populations. Thoma knew that detainees were given injections to put them into month-long comas, and saw with his own eyes that the people held there were as thin as he had been when he was in prison. Thoma took three packs of cigarettes with him whenever he visited so that he could give them to prisoners who would ask him for them, and said that he felt ill for weeks after each visit, images of those prisoners haunting him when he sat down at home with his family to eat.

It was only in 2012, 20 years after the "transition" to democracy, that the prime minister of Albania, Sali Berisha, formally acknowledged that the psychiatric hospitals of Elbasan, Korça and Berat were used as prisons and places of torture for political opponents of the regime, yet this was always informally known to Albanians, and certainly known to those who survived or who lost loved ones in these institutions. I have known people who survived the psychiatric hospital in various states of irreparable brokenness common to survivors of state torture. They were taken there for their perceived political and ideological opinions, and were those who could not be counted on to renounce their positions and accept fabricated charges in a public trial. In the mid-1960s, many Albanians were lured back from the diaspora in Australia, Canada, and the USA, only to be imprisoned in forced labour camps for political prisoners on their return. Some of these young men were later sent to the psychiatric hospital and many died there. From interviews with the family members of former internees who were close to some of the nurses who worked in this hospital, it is certain that detainees were continually drugged and restrained, essentially given psychiatric problems as torture, in this prison. None of the medical doctors who worked in Elbasan psychiatric hospital have ever been tried in a court of law, and at least one opened a private psychiatric practice in Tirana after the regime converted to capitalism in 1991.

From furniture collection, Thoma was moved to overseeing the collection of old clothes and the workshop of women who mended them for resale. Thoma saw being put in a workplace with women as a deliberate magnification of the chances of making a "mistake." Women, Thoma supposed, gossiped more than men and were more often recruited by the *Sigurimi* as low-paid informers, as they were eager to supplement child-rearing incomes. Then, as now, women were more often the ones to carry the economic brunt of single parenting, especially as the state largely denied that recalcitrant, roving, and violently raging husbands existed despite the moral whitewash of socialist society. With this in mind, Thoma was careful to avoid being alone with anyone who could fabricate charges against him, and was careful to maintain clear control of the books to avoid accusations of sabotage against the state, which carried a 20-year prison term. At this time, three *Sigurimi* men followed Thoma full time on rotating shifts. One took him aside and told him that there were three of them assigned to him alone, and that he should be careful – if he made a mistake he would be killed. Thoma took the man's revelation as an act of kindness rather than threat.

In 1967, all private property was prohibited and Thoma's family sold the last horses and sheep of the flock. Seventeen years later, in 1984, the state confiscated their family home to demolish it and build state apartment blocks. The state moved each son into his own small apartment with just his nuclear family, an attempt to weaken the trust between branches of the extended family and to enable easier state surveillance by neighbours and informers. Thoma often lost his temper at home in these hard years, and explained this as a consequence of knowing what the state could do to his family if they made any "mistakes." One day he returned home from work to find the children listening to the illegal Yugoslav channel on the radio, rather than the Albanian-sanctioned channels, which were the only legal radio stations. He told us how he flew into a rage and threw the radio to the floor. The children cried, and his wife shouted at him. "What are you doing? Are you crazy?"

"Have you been to prison? I've been to prison. I stayed there three months, tied up, with one potato to eat in the evening. They don't give you water, they drink it in front of you. I know how it is in a dungeon, so, I am not crazy," Thoma shouted.

Then he picked up the radio and it still worked, but the children didn't listen to foreign stations again. In re-telling the story, at the start he would be apologetic for his temper with the kids, but by the end he was sad, as if reliving the event, and still unable to understand how anyone could provoke attention that could have such dire consequences. His aim was to protect his family, yet only he knew the full extent of what he was protecting them from. This was a further wedge between them, and one common to many families where one person had been tortured and remained isolated with his or her knowledge of just how much damage the state was prepared to do. As specialists in the field of torture and trauma studies have widely noted, torture functions to encode the power of the state in the body of the victim, which they then carry with them into the wider world; the trauma can be triggered and lead to seemingly volatile or disproportionate reactions to small events, leaving the victim ashamed of their actions or alone with their returning memories.

Thoma's daughters finished the compulsory eight years of elementary school and then began to work. While Thoma ensured that his eldest son focused on study and went on to higher education, he decided that his daughters would be best equipped for the world by learning trades such as sewing and by working, which was also Vlach family tradition for women. For three years his daughters worked at home, in which time Thoma organized the materials for them to make carpets and couches, helping them at night. The carpets and couches were used as payments for favours and sold for cash to friends and networks that remained from the pre-communist times. People protected their social networks by never having coffee together in public, and by making their transactions at night or in places where surveillance could be thwarted. This illicit work worried Thoma, but he was driven by fear of another arrest and possible imprisonment, in which case his wife and family would need some savings to survive. In teaching himself and his daughters carpentry and sewing, Thoma also believed he was giving them a skill they could use for life, to support themselves despite regime changes. It wasn't that Thoma ever wondered if or when the regime would collapse, but that he knew one had to plan for survival because the future was unforeseeable.

Thoma described the period when they all worked illegally at home as "the great war," referring to inharmonious relations in the house and in the political sphere. He asked a friend with good connections, another ethnic Vlach, to personally approach a factory director and ask for positions for his daughters. In exchange he offered him their home-made carpets, but the friend was nervous about how to explain that he had any relations at all with Thoma, who had a bad biography. Thoma told him to say he was a cousin of his wife, who were also Vlach shepherds before the war. The director accepted them as workers, and so Thoma's daughters finally entered the state workforce.

Government surveillance under Enver Hoxha was total, and every aspect of life and time was dictated and controlled by the state. At least one person in every apartment block was an informant for the *Sigurimi* who monitored and reported on visitors, conversations and relationships. Albania is a small country, and as Thoma says, "If you farted in Elbasan they heard it in Tirana." People only met each other socially if their "biographies" aligned; if someone of "good biography" met with someone with a "bad biography" it could compromise their political reputation. The severe punishments for those meetings the state took exception to were enough to fuse people into awkward social isolation. One could be called to visit the police and explain what one had discussed with someone over coffee, and so meeting with people who were considered enemies of the state was to be avoided. It was also suspected that Albanians who had been abroad and returned to visit were actually agents of the *Sigurimi* themselves, and so these visitors were desperately avoided regardless of, and in fact precisely because of, how curious one might be to hear about the world outside isolated Albania. Thoma himself was approached and asked why he hadn't met with certain returning emigrants, and he replied that they were not his close family so he had no interest in meeting them. It was wise to avoid drinking in public as well, as waiters monitored how much you could afford to drink and this information could draw suspicion as to one's real black market income and result in interrogation.

In the 1960s, after breaking with Russia, it was commonly said that the number of informers for the *Sigurimi* increased from one in seven to one in every three. It was in these years that the *Sigurimi* attempted to recruit Thoma as an informer also. Two men that he didn't know visited his home and asked about his family, then they told him that they had a problem. This general language of threat clearly communicated the request. Do you care about your family, whom we are also watching, enough to help us solve some of our own state problems? Thoma said that he couldn't help them with problems as he was just working hard and looking after his own family only, and then he asked an old friend who was still connected to the Party if he could help him avoid repercussions for his refusal. This friend helped Thoma by informing to the *Sigurimi* himself that Thoma was "crazy" with nerves – that he was untrustworthy with anything more than his own job and suffered from a bad temper and kidney problems. This enabled Thoma's regime-long medical exemption from annual military conscription and forced labour, in addition to serving him well through conflicts with various institutions and people.

When speaking of his life between workplaces and under surveillance, Thoma also reminded us how popular he was with children for his ability to tell the stories of Nastradini, the clever fool character who appears throughout the Balkans in parables. The character of Nastradini speaks a truth through Thoma about living under powerful dictators and the constant threat of physical harm to one's family. One of Thoma's favourite Nastradini stories is the following:

> Nastradini was fooling people, so they told the sultan that he was a lazy man cheating them, and the sultan ordered his arrest and hanging. Two gendarmes went and arrested him at home, but on hearing the charge of hanging by the sultan, Nastradini said that he also wanted to take his donkey because Istanbul was a long way. As he was leaving, his wife told him, "O Nastradini Efendi, there in Istanbul they have good red cloth. Can you please bring me five metres to make a dress?"
>
> Nastradini thought, "I didn't know that my wife was so stupid. I am going to be hanged, and she asks me to buy things for her."
>
> Nastradini arrived in Istanbul, tied his donkey in the yard and then was taken before the sultan. The sultan asked, "Are you Nastradini?" and Nastradini answered, "Yes."
>
> "You lie to people," the sultan said.

"No," replied Nastradini, but the sultan insisted and Nastradini admitted that he lied to people. The sultan told him he would be hanged, and Nastradini replied that he had come to be hanged. Then the sultan told him: "If you can find the answer to these two questions, I will save your life."

"Fine," said Nastradini.

"Where is the middle of the world?" asked the sultan.

"That's where I have tied my donkey," said Nastradini.

"Good," said the sultan. "And how far is the Earth from the sky?"

"Ah", said Nastradini, "We need to measure this. Please give me a ladder, and then I will climb and measure it."

The sultan told him, "Bravo, you are very clever. You can go home." Nastradini took his donkey and went home. On the way he thought, "My wife was clever. She knew that I would come back, that's why she asked me for a dress."

This short parable tells us a lot about Thoma's ethic for survival: don't question whether the power is right or wrong, even and especially when it is one's very life which is at stake.

The *Sigurimi* controlled every aspect of employment and life in Albania, and directors in high positions gave privileged positions to *Sigurimi* informers and displaced those who refused to inform. If someone refused to work for the *Sigurimi*, they were often demoted to agricultural labour in the collective. Directors who failed to relocate workers in line with state requests were themselves relocated, so they often fired a group of workers to obfuscate the real targets of the attack, later moving those who were not being punished to a similar position elsewhere. This strategy maintained total confusion and inability to predict or ensure one's basic security in everyday working life under the regime. The *Sigurimi* would wait until the person deposed from his position was left unemployed and angry, and then would approach him or her again with an offer to work for them in return for a new workplace or a place in school for their children. If you spoke against the government in any way you were arrested under Article 12 of the Constitution – Agitation and

Propaganda – which carried a minimum sentence of 10 years. People were thus frightened into becoming informants and the whole society became more paranoid. It was a world in which there was no logic at all behind events of stunning cruelty other than individual machinations to maintain power at every level.

Thoma was painfully aware that his ability to refuse *Sigurimi* approaches was reliant on his ability to work illegally and save money, while avoiding the wrath of the Party. He also had extensive social and work networks. While Thoma himself was declared medically unable to attend the annual military training, *zbor*, or the regular forced labour events, called *aksion*, his wife and children participated in the multitude of state-designed public service duties that ensured limited free time. The working week was six days, and on Sunday the state often organized *aksions* – community public service labour. *Aksions* cleaned up the local area in working groups every Saturday morning, and were vital for larger projects such as helping with the harvest, digging terraces into mountains, painting slogans praising the Party, and building train lines and apartment buildings. Students at high school and university devoted whole months to these public service actions, while women and men who worked long hours in addition to looking after their families were also forced to participate.

After the split with China in 1978, militarisation intensified and Hoxha bombarded citizens with his paranoid propaganda of imminent invasion and decimation. Whether he believed it himself or not, everyday Albanians were victims of a decade-long relentless lie that they faced military attack from Greece, the USSR, the USA, and Yugoslavia in an ideological and potentially military sense. In preparation to defend their small nation from supposed invasion, 750,000 steel-reinforced concrete bunkers were manufactured and installed from the edge of the sea across the mountains, even as the lack of available food and shelter became dire. In many conversations, people have told me how isolated, poor and fearful life was then, and speaking today, they are often sad but never embarrassed at the absurd isolation that Hoxha forced them to live under; there can be no shame because there was simply no way to understand the absurd cruelty of Hoxha's system at the time. Even the most politically astute prisoners in the notorious Spaç prison, the men of those families purged from the inner ranks of the Politburo itself, believed Hoxha when he said that Albania's very existence as an independent nation was under threat.[4]

Everyday Albanians were not allowed to critically engage with the ideology and politics of defence, but were told to believe that national independence relied on total military mobilisation through ubiquitous slogans and military training. Schools and public buildings (which meant all buildings) were painted with slogans such as "We will fight," "Enver – Party," and, in the absence of a specific anniversary or event, "Thank you Enver." Enver Hoxha's portrait was in every school, hospital, shop and in very many peoples' homes – or at least in their front hall where neighbours could see it. *Zbor*, compulsory military training, took one to three weeks a year, and when it was your name on the list you had to leave your family and work and go to military camp, where you studied and practised equipment use and military strategy. Thoma's wife would come home exhausted and tanned by the work in the sun, and get right back into her work cooking and cleaning the home.

Contrary to what one might expect, elections held every four years were a day of state-orchestrated celebrations. There were speeches about the elections being free, unlike in other countries where the bourgeoisie bought votes, and there was a competition to see which region could complete the voting first on the day. Everyone in Elbasan voted before midday. The children sang and danced in their pioneer squads, and adults voted for Enver Hoxha and the Party; any alternative action would be easily recognized and punished. Dictatorship in this context relied on the practice of elections and voting, routine spectacles that forced individuals to demonstrate support for the regime. This meant that no one could blame others for creating their predicament. The people did indeed choose dictatorship, albeit in a setting of ubiquitous threat dressed in flowers and dancing that prevented people doing otherwise.

4   Fatos Lubonja, *Second Sentence* (London: I.B.Tauris, 2009).

The state controlled all media and information, and did its best to monitor everything that went on inside people's homes. Thoma often said that if one in every three people informed for the *Sigurimi*, who between himself, his wife, and his son, could be the informer? This rhetorical question highlighted the fear of the regime that pervaded family life at home. Thoma kept his family close in an attempt to prevent state infiltration and to protect them. State interference in private space was further extended with Hoxha's 1967 decree against religion. Hoxha declared that the religion of Albanians would be Albanianism, and he made the practice of religion illegal. The state confiscated churches and mosques, destroying them by using them as cow sheds, and vigilante youth went door-to-door collecting illegal religious icons to destroy. Thoma's mother did not want to destroy her icons, and so Thoma instructed her to hide them in the back of the closet and tell the visiting Party youths that her sons had already burned all her icons.

The personal was also the prerogative of the state in the most intimate of spheres: that of sex and childbirth. Contraception and abortion was illegal throughout the entire period – no condoms or contraceptive pills were imported, there was no education or available literature about the reproductive cycle, and people practised traditional methods of contraception such as withdrawal. As in Romania, this made physical intimacy fraught and served to keep relationships between people even more severely under pressure.[5] As abortions were illegal, women, nurses and doctors who assisted or performed abortions were put in prison as political traitors and seen as shameful by society, despite the stress for women of having to deal with so many births.

In 1974, with his other children finally in employment and as the paranoid isolationism of the regime made everyday acquisition of food a problem for everyone, Thoma's wife Maria fell pregnant again, at age 42. Maria's pregnancy became clear to Thoma from the way she suddenly became radiant and youthful. Considering their age and the fact

5   See Gail Kligman, *The Politics of Duplicity: Controlling Reproduction in Ceasescu's Romania* (Berkeley and Los Angeles: University of California Press, 1998).

one needed to queue for hours even to buy milk rationed for mothers, the pregnancy was a cause of upset as well as joy. Thoma and Maria approached a woman of Greek origin that Thoma had known for 18 years and whom he had observed being approached by young women for help, and she said she knew somebody who could help them with an abortion at a price. Thoma, however, knew from his female colleagues that numerous sudden deaths and disappearances of local young women were the results of clandestine abortions and suicides resulting from fear of pregnancy after romances and rape. He also knew of the women sentenced to prison for the crime of seeking or undergoing an abortion. Thus Thoma and Maria decided that the child would be born. This son grew up to come of age as the regime fell, and thus would be the only child of Thoma and Maria allowed to go on to higher education and university, also helping the family navigate the unforeseeable chaos of the 1990s.

* * *

In the last weeks of my time in Albania, I asked Thoma to bring some photographs that we could use in the book. On the day we met to look at the photographs, we also planned to photograph ourselves in the park. Thoma was waiting for us as we arrived, as usual, and had brought a nice tie with him to wear for the photographs. He also brought a few photographs of himself from different periods. Eda and I were shocked. In the photo of Thoma in Tirana after the war he looked happy, strong, and gallant, a well-dressed and self-confident young man. In all the photos taken after 1956, Thoma looked drawn, tense, and under great stress. He wasn't smiling, and the worry was etched in deep wrinkles on his face. His body was long and skeletal, his hands clasped his worry beads, and he appeared to be leaning against a wall to stay upright in one photo, a tightly folded bundle at a table in another. Thoma looked older in these photos from forty years ago than he did sitting before us in the park in 2010. How could the man we had come to know as larger than life, who we knew had survived communism through his adaptability, courage, humour and wit, look so scared and hungry?

It was suddenly clear – it was only now, in 2010 in a park in Tirana, that Thoma's memories became marvellous feats of his encounters with the communist regime. The parables of Nastradini escaping execution by the skin of his teeth, the cross referencing of God, Marx and Lenin, and the metaphors of the body as state to explain the *Sigurimi* fell into perspective – these were Thoma's internalised survival codes from a time that was unpredictable and dangerous.

Our work as a small group had been much more than the recounting of past events, it had given a meaning to our time together in the present, *against* the severe cruelties of the past. In his wonderful way of telling past experiences, Thoma brought his free self to stories of the times when he had been unable to act with any freedom at all.

Thoma Çaraoshi, 1980.

Thoma Çaraoshi.

Chapter Three

Stories to Make You Laugh and Cry
- Mevlude Dema

Gjergj Erebara, a journalist with a keen and vast knowledge of Albanian history, invited me to meet his Aunt, Mevlude Dema, for a coffee. At 9 a.m. on a quiet Sunday morning we met in the street outside the Ministry of Foreign Affairs on the Lana, the stream that runs from Dajti Mountain through the centre of Tirana at its foothills and further to the Adriatic Sea. Mevlude's sophistication in a creaseless blue cotton skirt-suit contrasted with Gjergj and I in our dishevelled early morning states.

The Ministry of Foreign Affairs was built by the Chinese government as their ambassadorial residence in 1972, and taken over by the Albanian government when they broke diplomatic ties with China in 1978. Next to the Ministry was one of the ubiquitous giant concrete apartment blocks built in the mid-1990s, and we sat in the first floor café, where the air was still smoky from the night before. Cafés are the primary entertainment and office space in Albania today. In many of the new apartment blocks, even in suburban areas, a vast space is allotted inside the building itself to a café, as well as smaller cafés and their plastic tables for clients on the dusty pavements outside. The décor of standard Italian black was a

dark contrast to the clear blue Tirana winter sky outside, and the young
waiters obligingly turned down the dance music, curious to overhear our
conversation. "Before the communists took it, this land belonged to my
family," Mevlude began, "so please feel here as if you are in my home."

Mevlude's parents both came from established Tirana families – families
that had lived in Tirana since it was just a small town 30 kilometres from
the ancient port city of Durres. Tirana was declared the capital city of
Albania at the Congress of Lushnja in 1920, and was further developed
as the capital under King Zog (1928–1939), then Italian (1939–1943)
and Nazi occupation (1943–1944). When the communists seized Tirana
in 1944 they recognized the threat that "real Tirana people" posed in
terms of economic and social capital, and worked hard to destroy these
old families, especially the intellectuals and land owners. In the socialist
period, it was difficult to gain permission to live in Tirana, and many
strove to live there as it was the heart of Albanian politics, power, and
social and cultural life. In post-socialist Albania, with massive population
movement into the capital city, the 'real Tirana people' have an image
of moral and cultural superiority and are known to have suffered at
the hands of the communists. Those who came to Tirana only in the
period after 1945 are not considered to be "Tirana people," but to be
of the cities and villages their ancestors came from before the regime.
Mevlude's family is one such family which have had their entire lives
controlled and influenced in minute detail by virtue of their esteemed
social position before World War Two.

Ramazan Dema, Mevlude's father, was an intellectual and one of the
founders of the education system in Tirana. An only son and orphaned
at age five, his uncle ensured he was educated at the American school
in Tirana, then in Elbasan and Istanbul. He lived and worked close to
his family in Tirana throughout the interwar governments of both Fan
Noli and King Zog, teaching for free and using his inherited wealth
to open new schools. He travelled to Italy and was well known in the
Albanian literary community. Mevlude's father stayed in Tirana for
the duration of World War Two and insisted on the message that "one
does not fight a war to gain profit from others." He was engaged in the

underground communist movement against fascist occupation, and in one family anecdote, Qazim Mulleti, a collaborator with the occupying forces and the Mayor of Tirana, called Ramazan for a meeting to discuss his opposition to the fascists. Mulleti offered Ramazan a gun, saying that if he escaped being killed by the fascists, he would still need to defend himself from the communists he sympathized with. Ramazan refused the gun, considering himself "a man of the pen, not of the gun." This position of non-violent independence has been passed down through the generations of the family.

Mevlude was born in 1942 and her mother did not work outside the home – it was unthinkable for women to pursue education and a career at that time – but she was literate and she read a lot. The family employed a nanny and a woman who did the housework. Mevlude's mother grew up behind what is now the Hotel Tirana International, and her five sisters married men from other established and respected Tirana families before the war. Her maternal grandmother lived with them too and was also literate and highly cultured. She went to the opera and theatre until she died at age 95 and she had travelled in Europe before the communist regime. She told Mevlude that, "if all the Adriatic Sea was ink and all the forests paper, still no one could record all the crimes the communists committed." Indeed, it was not just the theft of wealth but the exile from everything an open and cultural society had to offer which so persecuted those who were removed from the centre of Albanian society.

In 1947, Ramazan Dema ran as a candidate in the Albanian election without being a member of the Democratic Front, the largest organisation within the Communist Party of Albania, and for this he was arrested and tortured. The status of the Dema family in Tirana society could not be so easily forgotten, and Mevlude explained the importance of pre-war networks to survival even under the regime.

> My father was saved from execution because my mother's family knew the Kellezi family well. The Kellezi family heads were big traders before the war and shared a garden with my mother's family in that part of Tirana. Abdyl Kellezi, the youngest of the

brothers, studied economics in Italy, became a communist, and
was in the Political Bureau of the Party of Labor as Vice Chief of
the Ministerial Cabinet. Being a communist, he told the Party
where his own father had hidden the family gold and gave the
family's property to the state. When my father was arrested, my
grandmother contacted Abdyl Kellezi and asked him to save my
father from hanging. They tortured him for nine months anyway,
and when he returned from jail he didn't have any fingernails or
toenails. But my father was saved by that old friendship we still
had from before the communists. My father was a teacher, but the
communists sent him to work as a worker in a printing factory
here in Tirana. He died two years later.

Mevlude's maternal aunts had married into the old and well-known
Ndroqi, Basha and Pernaska families, whose sons had also married
young women of the Kellezi family. The Party purged these "old Tirana
people" almost immediately after the war, progressively confiscating their
property and gold, and persecuting the people in all facets of life. People
who were identified as not of the working class, as being bourgeois or land
owners, were "declassed" in the class wars. This did not mean that they
could be rehabilitated in the Albanian context. On the contrary, the status
of being "declassed," *deklasuar*, and the persecution which accompanied
living with this label, was passed on through the generations of a family.

By the time Mevlude was a teenager, all the aunts had been exiled
from Tirana to work in labouring jobs as punishment for their previous
status. One aunt (who had studied in Rome in 1947 and 1948) was
sentenced with her husband and Ramazan Dema, in the same group of
political representatives. This aunt was imprisoned for twenty years and
released in 1969. Others were sentenced to internal exile camps for work
in the region of Lushnje. The state exiled another of the aunts to Lushnje
without any documents or trial in order to seize her seven properties,
but she also appealed to personal pre-communist social connections
for her survival. She visited Beqir Balluku, also from a Tirana family,
and the Minister of Defence at the time, and told him that she had done

nothing against the communist government. He advised her to go back to Tirana and she did. She didn't live in her own house or work, but was nevertheless allowed to stay in Tirana rather than in rural exile under surveillance. This was possible in the first years of the regime as there was a population of just over 100,000 people in Tirana, a severe lack of literate and skilled Party of Labor members, and as a result a weak administrative and surveillance infrastructure compared to the years that followed.

The lives of Mevlude and her two brothers and five sisters were entirely dictated by their bad biographies as a declassed family. Mevlude was the only sibling who, through numerous twists of fate, was allowed to study at university, and her professional life was conducted under constant surveillance and threats. The personal lives of people were also dictated by their good or bad biographies in the eyes of the Party; the Party punished whole families, not simply individuals, and so a match made in marriage could provide leverage for upward mobility or persecution with very real material effects. In the 1950s, Mevlude read and reread a novel by German author Hans Fallada, entitled *The Postcard Game*. The story follows the activities of a family turning against Nazism in wartime Berlin, when having a family member in the Nazi party became vital for all aspects of life, and the existing moral and cultural values of the family in choosing intimate partners and friends were replaced by the definition of a "good family" as being a Nazi-associated family. To her teenage self, this claustrophobic novel seemed a map of the radical schism between the pre-communist and post-war moral and social landscape in Albania, and allowed her to hope that communism, like Nazism, would one day fall. It was exactly this clear recognition of the dictatorship as an externally imposed system that enabled Mevlude to live through relentless persecution as an "enemy of the state."

Between 1956 and 1958 Mevlude attended Qemal Stafa high school, the only high school in central Tirana, because the Party was desperate to educate people from all social strata, especially encouraging the education of girls. In 1955 Enver Hoxha made a speech at the Fourth Congress of the Women's Union of Albania in which he referred to women as "the proletarian of man" who had previously had "only one right: to bear children and to slave day and night."[6] Hoxha thus "liberated" women to the right to bear children, and to slave day and night both at home and for the state. The massive communist push for literacy and education was to create nurses, teachers and bureaucrats who could run the country as a modern state. Women remained the caretakers of each family and were still considered the property of their fathers and husbands, even as they fulfilled new roles working full time for the national economy. In Mevlude's words, reflective of the vocabulary available to describe society at the time, "the war of the classes did not yet have a consistent dynamic," meaning that the pre-socialist social structures still had value for individual and community relations. Mevlude's teachers were professionals who had been schooled abroad before the war. They knew who her father was, and they respected him.

Still, a student could not be given the highest grade unless they had achieved top results in the subject Doctrine and Propaganda of the Party of Labor. The students intuited that there was a lot at stake in this class. One of Mevlude's classmates once cried during a test in political philosophy, and when the professor asked her why she was crying, she answered that she was afraid of making a political mistake. Mevlude's parents did not openly tell the children that they were being forced to politically conform, or explain the dangers that could result from 'political mistakes,' for fear that such explicit conversation could lead to the children letting a dangerous opinion slip out in front of teachers or peers, leading to the further persecution of the entire family. Yet from the comparatively discouraging attitudes of her parents to the political subjects, Mevlude understood their political position and just how precarious their social place was. Children picked up on the silences and tensions at home and internalized the need to behave in a similarly defensive way at school even before they could put all the pieces of the puzzle together. Indeed, it was the unpredictability of communist policy and its implementation that kept people afraid and silent, or actively

6 *Selected Works of Enver Hoxha Volume 2,* 8 Nentori Publishing House, Tirana, 1975.

denouncing others as a pre-emptive defence strategy.

The Party assigned students to a profession when they came to the end of high school, and the timing was fortuitous for Mevlude. As she took her final high school exams, Professor Karajini from the State University of Tirana (only formed in 1957) visited the school to find students for the Faculty of Chemistry, set to open in 1958. Mevlude was chosen. Her family worried about what would happen when it came time to work in the industry, as professional positions were not allowed for "enemies of the state," but it was too good an opportunity to refuse. Throughout university Mevlude was aware of her status as a student with a bad biography, but with support from Semiramis Alia, the wife of Ramiz Alia, the Minister of Education and Culture between 1955 and 1958, Mevlude was protected from having her grades lowered in alignment with her "political" position in society. Semiramis Alia was not just the wife of a high ranking Politburo member, but also the daughter of Alexander Xhuvani, a leading intellectual of the interwar period after whom the Higher Education Institute in Elbasan was named when it opened in 1971.

Mevlude kept a low profile and was wary of friendships with peers. Even if someone did not know your biography it could cause problems for them to be seen with you, in addition to possibly causing problems for your own family if the new friend worked for or was interrogated by the *Sigurimi*. In the crowded student caféterias and dormitories, one revealed very little of one's personal biography for fear of political problems that could lead to expulsion and condemnation to a life of hard labour. In this way, self-censorship and distrust was made vital at the very moment and place that intelligent young individuals could pose the greatest threat to the dictatorship if they nurtured their natural curiosity and enthusiasm. Self-limitation for survival was at the heart of the most intimate friendships and was therefore replicated in the workforce, family and social life.

In this first generation of chemists, as the industry was just developing, students completed practical experience but were not sent to do "productive labour," the construction of roads and buildings. They

were still required to study "tactics of combat" (military theory) and
participate in the annual *aksion*, living with villagers for short amounts
of time while working in the fields. The state dictated where university
graduates of all courses would be sent to work, and Mevlude was first
assigned to work in the Institute of Chemistry Studies, but was moved
again to work in the factory with the worst reputation in the country,
the chemical factory of Tirana. It was a low professional position with
consistently paltry pay, but at least she could go home every evening and
she was never sent away from Tirana.

* * *

Due to her bad biography, Mevlude was not allowed to participate in any
State or professional events, and she was the object of constant suspicion
and surveillance. Her work included the first Albanian production of
washing detergent, and then paint, both of which were vital to everyday
life, yet she could not be acknowledged by name for her contributions. On
the positive side, she was also barred from political ideology lectures at
the factory and from doing overnight security shifts. Under the baseless
suspicion of potential sabotage, Mevlude could not attend state parades
and festivities, but had to hand out the paper flowers to workers to take
to the mass-choreographed events, making sure that all flowers were
returned the next day for future use. As a young, intelligent person, the
constant performance of social exclusion was painful and depressing,
even as she saw the absurdity of the choreographed collective celebrations.

On one occasion the resin in the factory caught fire and Mevlude
was denounced and discussed at the weekly Party meetings as possibly
responsible. She had no right to attend or defend herself at the factory
Party meetings, and although she was cleared of blame for the fire, she
was nevertheless disallowed from working alternate shifts. Every six
months the factory Party members updated her "characteristics file,"
a surveillance report in which enemies of the state were monitored by
their colleagues.

They wrote about how I behaved, what I wore, about my work, whether I had done research or not, and if I should continue to work in the factory or not. But some of my communist colleagues told me what was being said about me, because I was on good terms with them. One of my laboratory assistants once said in a meeting that I deserved a medal for my research studies, which by the way were modest, and the next morning she was removed from being a Party member and sent to work as a common worker on the factory floor.

Albanian society was a kind of forced collectivism under the communist regime. Everyone knew they were being watched, and being alone opened someone to accusations of individualism and "shunning the collective spirit." Mevlude had the enforced space to be alone and to think, but the exclusion was a "form of moral torture," as the state intended and so Mevlude focused solely on her professional life in order to survive.

My profession – this is what my life has revolved around. It was all I had! People in the factory would tell me not to participate in research because the Party would not credit my work. Very often my name was not mentioned on the studies I did, but I didn't let that stop me. My life was going to the library, reading, writing, translating. No one came to visit, even if someone wanted to visit I told them not to come. My colleagues, even communists, respected me and would ask me why I worked when I would not be credited, but work was my life and it still is.

On the other hand I would not let any cultural event pass and I attended the lectures of my brother in law, Gëzim Erebara, in the Academy of Arts. I was very engaged with culture.

If you had a bad biography it was like you had leprosy: nobody visited your house, even relatives, because they were afraid. In my personal life it was the same. I could only marry a worker. If I had married an engineer I would have been exiled to a village, interned. A former prisoner convicted of stealing asked me to marry him, but I said no because I was not from the same place as him, although we both had a bad biography. I was persecuted politically but not morally, so I decided to stay alone.

Mevlude often prefaced her stories with the warning that they could make you laugh and cry at the same time. In 1976, Mevlude discovered how to restore the properties of a vital chemical that could not survive the three month voyage from China. The Party secretary of Tirana came to the factory and called her, but, as she wasn't allowed to approach Party members, she thought he was calling someone else "Comrade Engineer." When she understood he really did intend to speak to her, he and the factory director congratulated her for the achievements and the Party secretary said that she would be rewarded with a special mention in the Women's Congress. When the day arrived and they were listening to the Congress on the radio at work, Mevlude was indeed mentioned – but not by name, only as "Chemical Factory Engineer." The petty attention to detail required for such blunt violence is so incongruent that both laughter and tears spring to the eye.

On the following "Innovator's Day," 11 September, the Party gave Mevlude a photograph of Enver Hoxha as recognition for her work. This sparked alarm in the family because if anyone from the Party visited the house they would find no communist books, medals or photos of Enver Hoxha on the walls (as had become vital in private homes as well as public buildings). Mevlude thus stuck the unwelcome gift on the wall in the front corridor where anyone, such as local Party representatives or *Sigurimi*, coming to the door would see it. When her brother arrived home that evening he said, "Enver has no place in our house!" and tore the photo into pieces. Terrified about how to dispose of the pieces (which could bring a 10-year prison sentence), Mevlude and her brother carried them in their pockets and threw them away in distant and different parts of the city so as not to be discovered. They threw some pieces into the Lana River near where we drank our coffee; others they threw piece by piece into rubbish bins on the main streets of Tirana.

In the factory, colleagues denounced each other for a variety of reasons. Sometimes they were paid informants of the *Sigurimi*, sometimes they were acting on a personal grudge, but denouncing someone was also a way to show vigilance and commitment to the Party. One factory engineer was openly denounced by a colleague for sitting on the daily state newspaper *Zeri i Popullit* (Voice of the People) where there was a photograph of Enver Hoxha. The accusation was made at a Party meeting in the factory and very nearly went to the central committee for trial. On another occasion, a young unmarried couple who had recently fallen in love were seen embracing in the factory. Two days later, the factory director announced their engagement, without the consent of the family or the couple. Mevlude pointed out that while there was a rhetorical Party push for women to be educated, independent and working, traditional Albanian values that enforced marriage were combined with the illegality of contraception and family planning to closely control the lives of young people. The communist discourse of women's emancipation brought women into the workforce, but they were still often forced into marriage and childbirth. There was no movement to bring men into the field of housework or to address the high levels of normalized domestic violence used by husbands as a form of control.

By 1967, clergy of all religions had long been executed or imprisoned, so teachers and factory directors were used to implement the "war against religion." Factories provided meat and drinks for workers during Lent and Ramadan to test who was fasting for religious reasons. Meat was especially difficult to refuse when it cost so much in the market. On feast days for Christians and Muslims, teachers would ask students whose mother was cooking baklava at home, the special food for such celebrations. On one small Eid, a teacher asked Mevlude's niece why her grandmother was making baklava, and she said that she didn't know. The school was close to the house, so in the break she asked her grandmother, who told her that the baklava was for Mevlude's birthday. This was what she told the teacher. Two months later the family again made baklava for Eid, and when the teacher asked the child why they had baklava this time, she answered that it must be Mevlude's birthday again, causing much laughter and anxiety when she recounted the conversation at home.

In addition to constant surveillance at schools and workplaces, the *Sigurimi* had paid informers living in every street and block, referred to as "50 lek," the negligible amount the state paid for their services. These informers also asked others to work for the *Sigurimi*, especially those with "bad biographies," as a way for them to redeem themselves in the eyes of the state. When the neighbourhood informer asked Mevlude to write reports for them, she replied that she would have no one to report on as, he had seen for himself, no one visited the family home and she did not socialize with non-family members.

One thing Mevlude was not exempt from was the 20 days of military training each year called *zbor*. All Albanians (except those with personal connections or medical problems), both male and female, had to attend the trainings, which were centrally organized and impossible to reschedule – even if it clashed with one's wedding day. According to the law, anyone with a university education was an officer, but Mevlude was not entitled to this ranking because of her bad biography. In groups of 300 to 800, participants would be given state-owned military uniforms (that often did not fit the individual), shoes and weapons. If there were not enough real rifles, women were given wooden rifle-shaped sticks instead of real ones. Participants slept in bunk beds in unheated barracks, ate gruel and watery soup with beans, dug their own pit toilets, and washed their clothes in local streams, if at all.

There were no showers, only running streams (unless they were frozen over). Many women I spoke to laughed in sad disbelief when they remembered the conditions they experienced at *zbor*, and many also commented that it was a miracle more people didn't contract severe infections from the unhygienic conditions. In fact, many cases of chronic pneumonia resulted from the unprotected conditions.

The military training of the *zbor* was seriously planned by army tacticians, but was often considered farcical and useless as military training by participants on the ground. People did recognize, however, that the function of *zbor*, as with the *aksion*, was to monopolise the time and energy of the population. The weapons were old, and despite the intense state propaganda about imminent military invasion, Albanians who were hungry, cold and witnessing the lack of technology first-hand were not at all convinced that they could defend the country from invading American, Russian, Yugoslav or Greek forces. They were convinced by example, however, that one would be sent to prison for anti-state propaganda if caught laughing out loud or refusing to participate. After the break with China, Hoxha's paranoid militarism reached extraordinary heights with the construction of bunkers, even as food availability continued to drop. In their small trusted family groups, some people discussed just how much the military delusions were costing the state.

Until 1978, Chinese chemists worked in Mevlude's laboratory alongside the Albanian staff. Communicating in Russian, they shared a lot of jokes, specifically about what clothing they were not allowed to wear, as vigilance against foreign influences in dress intensified after 1974. Taking many ideas for punishment and control from Maoist China's Cultural Revolution, Enver Hoxha's Cultural and Ideological Revolution in Albania also attacked "imperialist influences." The Chinese chemists would borrow Mevlude's modestly heeled shoes and parade in the laboratory; someone would impersonate the Chinese supervisor arriving on the scene, and everyone would laugh hysterically and throw off the shoes. In reality, being caught wearing heeled shoes would have resulted in punishment for the Chinese chemists.

The Chinese workers were not supposed to socialize with the Albanian workers and they were accommodated in a hotel under constant surveillance. Yet on one occasion, Mevlude invited the Chinese colleagues to her brother's wedding without telling them where they were going, so as not to alert the authorities, and to avoid obliging them to buy a gift. She laughed to recall the stunned faces of her colleagues finding themselves in the middle of an Albanian wedding being photographed with the bride. They were touched by the rare gesture, and they put photographs of the event on the walls of the laboratory. Mevlude's friendships with these women feature prominently in her stories of her workplace, perhaps because they were even more irredeemably outsiders than she was herself.

In 1978 Albania severed all ties with China, and the Chinese chemists simply didn't come to work one day. No one had a chance to say goodbye, and the director took down the photos from the laboratory walls.

* * *

The catastrophe in my life started in 1977; my brother disappeared while trying to escape from Albania. We don't know if he is alive or not, even today, or whether he was killed. He just disappeared. He was living with me, but he didn't talk with anyone about an escape plan, it was a surprise to us. The investigating officer called me to his office and screamed that I should publically disown him for his act. They said that he tried to swim to Yugoslavia across Lake Ohrid from Pogradec. This was what they said, officially, but nobody knows what really happened. There is no record of what happened to his body. I was terrified, but I told the investigator that I would not disown him, that whatever happened he would continue to be my brother. He told me that he would break the desk of his office on my head and deport me to a village if I didn't disown him. The government wanted to forcibly relocate us, and we didn't know what to do with the library, which was full of yellow books [illegal books]. All those yellow books!

Just the day before her brother's disappearance, the director at the factory had nominated Mevlude for promotion to head engineer, and Mevlude believes that it was due to her professional value to the state that she was not internally exiled. Needless to say she was not promoted, and her salary was cut from 780 to 730 lek a month. At this time bread cost 5 lek, a litre of milk was 5 lek, butter was 5 lek per 100g, meat was 22 lek per kg and walnuts were 100 lek per kg. Each of these products, however, were severely rationed, and could only be purchased when one had a ration card called a *tollon*, which were allotted by the state at a set rate per family, regardless of the size of the family. The ration for milk was one litre per week per child, but one had to queue with the child in hand in order to use the *tollon*. Queues for milk and eggs in Tirana and other large cities began at 4 a.m. due to limited availability. In addition to memories of strange questions about baklava, many who grew up in Albanian cities in the 1980s remember being woken to go to the milk queue, wrapped in blankets, before sunrise.

After the disappearance of her brother, Mevlude became even more socially and professionally isolated. The trauma of his disappearance made keeping up appearances torturous, and the pain of the loss is evident even today, worsened by the refusal of post-socialist regimes to disclose what actually happened. Twenty-five years later there have still not been any government programs to systematically resolve cases of disappearance and execution. People who have not known the fate of their loved ones for so long are often afraid to find information because they know that there is no source that can be fully trusted. As we will see in the following chapters, government records were often written in total independence of the truth or actual events in order to suit the requirements of the regime. Following her brother's disappearance, the police searched the house and confiscated all items they considered valuable – old gold coins, heirlooms and books. One of her sisters broke contact with the family in order to give her children a chance to have good biographies and thus be able to access higher education.

Mevlude continued to work despite the trauma of losing her brother. She was an external teacher of chemistry at the State University of Tirana due to the continuing support of Semiramis Alia, supervising students on practical work experience in the factory. She completed all necessary exams and requirements for her PhD, but the University would not award her the degree. In the 1980s, Albania's self-isolation from all international allies made everyday life even harder. In education, the right of students in the Party to criticize teachers overtook the respect for knowledge which had been present twenty years earlier. One of Mevlude's colleagues from the factory was sent to teach in the school for mechanics, and he lost his patience with a student interrogating the political ideology behind the lesson, pointed to the picture of Enver Hoxha on the classroom wall and said, "It's not your fault, but his, who lets you judge me as you wish." He was exiled to work in the mines. The worsening food shortages made people desperate and employees in the chemical factory, as in every other workplace, stole materials to exchange with products from other nearby factories, such as dairy products and vegetables from greenhouses. When Mevlude turned a blind eye to this, she was criticized in the Party meetings for failure to be vigilant and protect state property.

The lack of any international allies to supply materials was a chronic problem for industry in all fields. On one occasion, the chemical factory called the 27 engineers, except Mevlude, to a meeting. There was a problem. The nature of the problem was treated as a secret of national security, which could not be shared with anyone who had a "stained" biography, such as Mevlude. When they couldn't solve the problem, however, one of Mevlude's colleagues asked her for help.

> When they called me, I asked for three days to experiment in the Laboratory. I worked for 48 hours and solved the problem, then the information was sent to the Party Committee that I had sabotaged the state because I hadn't given the research solution earlier. The director criticized me in his office, but I replied that I had learnt of the problem on Friday, asked for the raw materials and given an answer by Saturday. How could I have withheld prior research when I didn't know what they were researching? They wanted to humiliate people, to make people afraid so they wouldn't dare to do anything against the system.

When Enver Hoxha died in April 1985, workers from all over the country visited his body while it was held in state. Footage available online, which was recorded at the time for television broadcast, shows a massive public expression of grief in the queues to visit the body. However, not everyone felt a sense of loss at Hoxha's death. When Mevlude was forced to visit his coffin with everyone from the factory, she passed near his body and said in her mind, "Finally I get to see you dead." In the Dema family that day there was a genuine sense of happiness and celebration. One of her friends, however, had a son born on that date, and she had to hide the birthday cake she had cooked for him for fear that the son would mention the cake at school and raise suspicion that the family was celebrating Hoxha's death.

I heard similar stories to this one from many people, and it was widely feared that one's action could be read as being anti-regime. Of course, it was precisely because everyone had critical thoughts against the regime that people could easily accuse others of the same thing. The system relied on a culture of constant criticism and counter-criticism framed as class war, which was in fact people motivated to denounce others before they could be denounced themselves.

* * *

As the "class war eased" in 1991 under the post-Hoxha rule of Ramiz Alia, and due to student protests and international pressure for reform, Mevlude was able to step up and take her place as a recognized professional in the factory.

> I secretly took my characteristics file from the factory in 1991 because after that they burnt everything. I saved my folder, I have it in the library at home. I took the pages I needed and I have read what they wrote there about me. Once, in the 1990s, I met the human resources officer, a woman, in the bus. During my years at work in the factory I supervised almost all the young engineers in their dissertations. When I say supervised, I mean that I read line by line all the dissertations, especially as my name could have been written there and I was afraid I'd be humiliated if it was discovered. The human resources officer had written with handwriting in one of the pages in my folder that I did not help the young engineers. When I saw her in the bus, I asked her why she had written that when she knew very well that I always helped them. Her face flushed; she said she hadn't written it. I told her that I cannot forget her handwriting, and she got off the bus. Anyway, I cannot blame her – circumstances were difficult back then.

Such sympathy for people who informed or acted against them is common amongst the formerly politically persecuted, but harder to deal with is how those who collaborated with the regime against them have rationalised their actions and often failed to acknowledge the damage they did.

> Here is a story to make you laugh and cry at the same time. You know I had a lot of experience in the company, more than 30 years of work experience, but when the foreign specialists visited us they were accompanied by a young engineer who was married to a deputy named Ethem Ruka. They were usually German specialists, but I was not allowed to meet them. The young engineer did not have the necessary experience and could not answer all the questions asked by the foreign experts, so she used to call up to me on the third floor from the ground level to ask me, "Mevluuuudeeeee, what can I say about this?" This happened many times, but after Ramiz Alia started to ease the class war in 1991, I was allowed to meet and accompany the foreign specialists in the factory for the first time. One German specialist stood up in the meeting and said that for three years he had wondered what "Mevlude" meant in Albanian, but he had never thought that it could be a person.
> The director said, "She has a bad biography, and because of this she couldn't meet you."
> He could say it so simply! That really hurt.

In 1991, Mevlude was included for the first time in a delegation visit from the factory to Germany and Hungary.

> When we were in Germany, one of my colleagues who had suffered a lot, like me, told the director of the company that in Albania we were still eating with rations, such as 100 grams of butter per week for five people. At the end of the farewell ceremony, the German director asked one of the women from the company to collect all

the leftovers from the tables and give them to us to take them to Albania. I felt very bad. It was our reality, but it was such a big offence. Foreigners cannot imagine how we lived, what we had to suffer. When I was in Sarajevo in 2001 I couldn't stop crying, even after the war it was better there than here.

* * *

Those who were powerless at the time of socialism's collapse in 1991 are still, overwhelmingly, politically, bureaucratically and economically marginalized and even persecuted today. The private property taken by the former regime has not been reinstituted or systematically compensated for, even as former communists and contemporary politicians have allowed housing and business developments throughout Albania. Land restitution claims languish in drawn out court trials where judicial outcomes can be bought. In the course of our first conversation, Mevlude said, "My life is a life without meaning," meaning that there is no conclusion of moral justice in the chronology of a life lived under the control of the communist regime. Survival of constant exclusion does not have a moral meaning unto itself. Many people have told me the same thing, that there is no reward for suffering, no valour in surviving persecution; there is pain. I asked Mevlude how she has survived the heavy sadness of those decades, of these decades, and she answered that books have been her refuge, literature, professional translation, and study, as well as family, art, and opera.

Mevlude lived in the physical centre of the regime. The city of Tirana, as with the lives of its citizens, was concretely transformed and determined by the communist regime. The part of the centre where the Party Politburo lived, known as "the block," was off limits to outsiders and bordered with armed guards. The leaders of the proletariat slept, interrogators tortured, and *Sigurimi* officers drank coffee in the nationalised homes of the established families they had imprisoned, exiled and executed. Public spaces were marked by queues, streets without cars where workers crammed into crowded buses, and the slogans of the regime written

on the walls. But Mevlude's world transcended the physical, her world
was her profession, the world of culture, and her family. In our final
interview I wanted to bring Mevlude's world back to the city and the
acts of everyday resistance that she had shared with me in her stories.
I brought a fold-out street map of Tirana and handed her a pen, asking
her to show me her city, to mark the map of her world.

I put the pen down on the spot where we were sitting and circled the
paper.

"Where is your house?" I asked her.

Her pen hovered over the map, then made the slightest mark on
the paper.

"And the university?" Again, with a slight mark,

"And your factory?"

She took the map, turned it – her fingers traced roads, past the train
station, north-east, the industrial sector.

"It's here," she circled in the air above the map.

"Could you mark the place?"

She drew a careful outline, small. It was an exact shape – the
asymmetrical perimeters of the factory building. In proportion.

"Where was the dairy factory where the workers exchanged chemical
products for food?"

Two blocks west, there she drew, again, a perfect light-lined bird's-eye
view of the building.

Sitting there at our last coffee together, Tirana redrawn, Mevlude told
me a joke.

> Once a group of Party leaders went to a village. There was
> a communist song about Enver Hoxha and the fight of the
> communist partisans in the Second World War entitled "Who
> Brought the Partisans to Us!" In this village there was an old man;
> he had once been the richest man in the village, but by this time
> he'd long been a worker and an outsider, considered a madman.
> The Party leaders started to tease him, "Come on old man, sing

us a song!" And the old man answered, "Alright then, let's sing 'Who the hell brought those Partisans to us?!'"

Tirana today: View of the Lana river up to Mt Dajti, Tirana, Spring 2012.

Chapter Four

Just One Moment Can Break a Soul
- Diana Keçi

I'd heard about Diana long before I met her. American Peace Corp volunteers I'd met throughout the years had told me that Diana was the person they turned to for explanations of how things worked in Albanian society. One day I ran into a former Peace Corp volunteer who asked me if I had ever heard Diana sing the Maoist songs she learnt from her Chinese teachers of English at the State University of Tirana in the 1970s. I had not. I called her for a coffee.

In our first of four long meetings at the bustling café called Taiwan, beside the Lana, I easily understood how Diana was so loved and respected. An attentive conversationalist with a strong and steady energy, Diana listened to people's opinions and then contributed to the discussion with anecdotes from her own personal experience, synthesising emotion and analysis. Diana's presentation of the critical moments in her life showed that she had always tried to understand herself and the world around her, and she embraced our meetings as a space to reflect on her experiences as one individual amongst many in socialist society.

In a café, people would stop by the table to greet Diana and she always responded with a genuine happiness to see them and an interest in their lives. After introducing me and explaining what we were talking about, she would include them in a memory. "Remember when we sang Italian songs around the fire at night during *zbor*? Remember when we all queued for milk before dawn?"

People clearly loved to be around her, and Diana's sincere inclusiveness deeply influenced her own interpretations of their actions. We spoke at length about the specific problems facing women in patriarchal Albanian society – both then and now – and about how the Party treated individuals differently depending not only on their political status but also, always, according to their gender and ethnicity.

* * *

Diana was born in 1960 in Durres, where her mother worked at a child care centre for new-born infants, and her father worked as an economist for the agricultural bank, and later for the Port Authority. "We were a very artistic family. There were five of us children in our small two-room house, but it seemed big enough to me then. Every night we would sit together. My brother had a guitar, my father knew the lyrics of songs, we sisters could sing, and my mother would pick up another instrument." The siblings played together and with friends at the local beach through the long hot summers.

From the windows of her family house in Durres, Diana could see the Faith Mosque, built in 1503, and the call to prayer was part of the neighbourhood soundscape. Then in 1967, at the start of Diana's first year of school, the mosque remained dark and there was no call to prayer for the celebration of Eid. In February Enver Hoxha had declared that all mosques and churches that had not been confiscated with the Agrarian Reform Law of 1945 were now closed. Diana entered school in this first year of Albania's official policy of atheism, and the curriculum was explicitly anti-religion, intent upon educating young people as model Party activists. Hoxha's dictum that the religion of Albanians was Albania was taught to all children from 1967 onwards.

By the time children entered the first grade they were familiar with the monistic structure of Albanian society. They were used to photographs of Enver Hoxha in health clinics, libraries, bread shops and kindergartens, as well as on billboards, placards and the front pages of newspapers and magazines. Slogans declaring love and gratitude to Enver and the Party were written in curvaceous or commanding blood red script on freshly whitewashed walls throughout public space. Even if children couldn't read or write themselves, the slogans were most likely familiar to them through Party publications for children and storybooks.

> It was a different culture then. People read books, novels, everything! Yes, all of my family loved to read, except for my brother, who liked football more. We all read the one copy of *Fatosi* [the monthly publication for primary school children] because if one kid at school had it, then we all wanted it. We bought it or borrowed it from a friend. And there were very good libraries, I would go and read there or take a book home with me. The librarian was lovely and took great care of the books. She helped kids to choose the books. She'd say, "Oh, *The Three Comrades* is good for you. You've read it? Then take this one," and all the kids knew the books. Then in literature classes we were assigned books to read, and we would discuss the deeper meanings.

Universal literacy was one of the Party's claims to success. Diana remembers the stories about brave socialist comrades, but also that there were no books about life in other countries. Diana's generation were born into established socialist society, and the Party controlled every element of a child's education and socialization. These kids grew up not knowing anything other than socialist rhetoric and concepts, sometimes to the dismay of their parents.

> I had a revolutionary spirit, even in kindergarten. I didn't want my mum to dress me in beautiful white dresses for Bajram – Eid as we call it now – so I told her that I would "do a Datsi Bao," against

her, which was a Chinese revolutionary action, because she followed religion. And I made my dress all dirty, covered with dirt, because I didn't want to be a religious person. Oh my God, I was so revolutionary! My mother couldn't do anything. She just said, "Oh Diana, so this is who you are!"

Parents walked a fine line in moments like this, aware that their children had no knowledge of what existed before or outside communist doctrine, and also that they lived in a new world in which children could innocently report their actions at home to teachers or informers. In the fifth grade, when students joined the Pioneers, mothers sewed red scarves and found red plastic toggles for students to wear over their white shirts at school assembly each morning. Standing to attention, students shouted together "Pioneers of Enver, you are ready to fight for the Party! Always ready!"

The Party also organised summer camps for young children, ensuring that they had fun in supervised settings when school was closed. This enabled parents to continue work uninterrupted and children to be ideologically educated in their leisure time. The camps were great fun for the children who could afford to go and who were not excluded due to being from politically persecuted families.

You paid a very small fee and went with your friends away from your family for two weeks. We had fun. Playing guitar, meeting with friends. I went to Pogradec when I was 12, not even in high school, and there were children there from our neighbourhood, and my brother was at another camp and we saw each other in passing buses, and I just put apples in a bag, a cloth bag, because we didn't have plastic bags, and I gave it to my brother and everyone said, "Sisters are so good to brothers!" It was so organised. I was a child, and it was great to be around people, concerts, songs, dancing, reciting poetry, so many activities! It was very beautiful. I have nostalgia for that time because you were on your own, and your mother would come to see you with a bit of food at every Pioneers camp. A lot of small pieces of life created your personality.

You felt more responsible because you were on your own and you gained a trust from your parents that you realise later really helps you. We were five children, very poor, but every year one of us at least would go away. And now there is nowhere you can send your children safely with a purpose.

Even when it was not my turn to go to a camp, we organised every day to go to Durres Beach, took bread and tomatoes, and just played all day at the beach. Beautiful. It was a very important foundation for your personality – you had a sense of being in another environment.

The Party thus defined and policed what could be read or studied about the world, but Diana's words highlight how this control enabled those with good biographies to feel safe in the structured patriotic activities. For children and young adults, group holidays were exciting, and they expressed their love of country and friends while basking in the promise that the omnipresent Uncle Enver would protect and watch over them. Students with bad biographies were not at the camps, of course, they were scapegoated as examples of the dangerous enemies amongst the people.

Constant reports of external threats against Albania's very existence mobilized patriotism in the passionate youth. In the 1940s and 1950s, Hoxha had successively broken with Yugoslav and Russian communist allies, and in the late 1960s he intensified paranoia that the USA, USSR or Greece could invade Albania from the sea, land and air. The military defence of Albania became a national priority and all citizens were prepared to fight. The army built tunnels and bunkers throughout the country for night raid simulations. The Italians had invaded Albania through the ports, including Durres, in 1917 and in 1939, and so it was a major site of military fortification against invasion by sea in the communist period. Alarms and loudspeakers were mounted throughout the city, and verbal communication from Party leaders in each neighbourhood or apartment block told people when to stay home and blacken the windows or go to the designated bunker at the sounding of the alarm.

On the days when there would be a practice evacuation, information was passed by word of mouth about the time that the sirens would sound. One kind of siren meant evacuation, and families had to go to the bunkers or tunnels below the apartment blocks within two or three minutes. As Diana remembers, "Everyone was talking. It was cold, it was night, sometimes at midnight or 1 a.m., just as you were almost asleep in bed. But we usually came home again quickly, and everyone took it positively, saying, 'The Party has a reason to prepare us for war.' You believed what you were told because it was like a hammer in your brain – it happened all the time." If the alarm was to stay home, families darkened the windows. The bunkers seemed cavernous to Diana as a child, but she realized in the 1990s, when people discussed what to do with the bunkers, that the largest of underground tunnels was only the size of two parked cars. This could not have been realized by Diana as a child, of course, because privately owned cars were not allowed in Albania, and so there was no need for garages. Most families lived in spaces approximate in size to a double garage.

With high grades, a clean political biography, and a revolutionary spirit, Diana was accepted into the Asim Vokshi Middle School for Foreign Languages in Tirana, where they taught English, French, Russian and Latin. From age 14, she commuted from Durres to Tirana for school. Her mother woke her each morning at 5 a.m., and sent her to the train station with a hard-boiled egg.

> All my life my mum said, "Oh Diana, Diana. You made me wake up so early in the morning every day of my life – I woke up every morning for you."
> "Oh Mum," I said, "don't do that to me!"
> I woke up at 5 a.m. and I carried in my hands a boiled egg, which had two functions: to keep my hands warm and to eat for my breakfast. Eggs were cheap and the train to Tirana took one hour and fifteen minutes.

With her monthly travel ticket, Diana enjoyed the bustle of the train ride along with many other students. The train guard would whistle the time of punctual departure, and the carriages filled with the sound of Radio Tirana broadcasting songs with lyrics about everyday life as well as working songs from the co-operatives, all written in the socialist period. The Tirana–Durres trains were crowded and lively, especially when Party workers going to or returning from a short vacation in one of the workers' resorts on the coast travelled with everything they needed for their vacation. The rooms of the so-called resorts were empty, so vacationers took their own gas cookers, chairs, tables and food, and all were passed from the platform, through the train windows, and stuffed into the overhead racks.

In high school, Diana became a Pioneer commandant, leading hundreds of students on daily assembly with the chant of *Always Ready!* Students recited a dedication to mobilize themselves and study hard for the Party, and stated that the Party was their mother and Enver their father. Diana was careful not to trip in her oversized shoes handed-down from her sister, her only pair. But these things didn't feel like poverty or oppression. Diana's youthful energy was dedicated to study and the Party, and there was a strong camaraderie amongst those who were considered the best of the new generation. They believed in their work to make Albania a better place.

Later, in high school, Diana participated with the many other students of Tirana in the choreographed street parades on 1 May and 28 November, the same parades that those with bad biographies, such as Mevlude, were not allowed to attend. For weeks in advance, students practised their choreographed parts during school hours, and Diana marvelled during our conversations at the enthusiasm that enabled children to physically rehearse for hours on end with only an egg at 5 a.m. as sustenance.

The parade footage and photographs online today testify to the mobilization of all levels of Albanian society to perform total commitment to Enver Hoxha and the Party. School children performed in the stadiums and on the streets along with thousands of factory workers, the military, police and emergency services. The Party also curated and policed the crowds to fill grandstands and line the boulevards with appropriate attire and expressions. The film footage, even in the years when isolation had dire consequences on everyday lives, shows women, men and children glowing with excitement and fervour. For many, the pleasure of the dictator's benevolent recognition was a more powerful emotion than anger at the fact that Party members ate and dressed much better than the workers they claimed to champion. In any case, those who felt anger at the regime knew that to show it would lead directly to prison, and so they lived, as Diana described it, in two contradictory worlds.

Diana's entire education and social world revolved around dedication to the Albanian nation as inseparable from Enver Hoxha and the Party. Diana's father watched Hoxha purge popular artists and trusted Politburo members, espousing the path of international isolation called "self-reliance." He began to talk about political ideology and economic practice to Diana at home, and invited her to listen in secret with him to Elez Biberaj on the radio. On Tuesdays, Thursdays and Saturdays, Biberaj announced uncensored world news on *Voice of America* from his studio in Washington DC, putting Albania in an international context.

1 May Parade, Tirana 1983.

Sherif Keçi, Diana's father, had worked for Koci Xoxe, the Minister of Defence and the Minister of the Interior. Xoxe had warned him to leave the job or face persecution as factional divides within the Party became evident in the late 1940s, but Sherif refused to leave his workplace. In 1949 Hoxha accused Xoxe of deviationism and of plotting with Yugoslav agents against the Albanian Party of Labor, and he was executed in June 1949. Diana's father survived the purge and was sent to work as an accountant at the Port. He waited until his children were old enough to understand that what was spoken at home should not be spoken outside, and then passed his knowledge on to them. He spoke Italian and understood economic theory from his pre-war studies, and he told his children why life in Yugoslavia was freer than in Albania and why self-reliance was impossible for a country as small as Albania.

Still, Diana reflected, the everyday news was totally controlled by the Albanian state, and the entire language of all spheres of life revolved around reliance on the Party, so when she heard Biberaj's program on *Voice of America*, she suspected that he was a foreign propagandist manipulating Albanians. She could not easily conceive of the entire state apparatus of Albania manipulating the people to maintain control. She loved and respected her father, and saw the logic in what he said, but was terrified that he spoke so openly against the Party and socialism, which she had not only believed in until then, but knew she would have to demonstrate belief in at school and in all relations with the outside world. Diana marks this moment, in the middle of high school, as when she began to live two separate realities.

Diana told me about hearing Elez Biberaj speak, in person, to English teachers in Tirana in the early 1990s. Diana assembled with hundreds of her peers in the pyramid-shaped building in central Tirana built as a museum to Enver Hoxha after his death in 1985. Biberaj's voice had taken her right back to the intimate and dangerous feeling of listening to the radio programs with her father, unsure of whom to believe. Sitting in the café Taiwan, Diana told me that when Biberaj began to speak her tears had flowed. She began crying again in the café as she recounted the event.

When I looked around me, many other teachers were sobbing too.

This was the voice that had been telling the truth! I knew this voice so well! All those years when I had doubted both my father and the state, he was telling us the truth! We cried then because we had lost decades and there was so much persecution, and it was all shown to be for a government that lied to us and controlled us! Oh, we cried that day, I cry even when I remember!

I did not know yet what Diana had experienced, but I understood that this anecdote communicated a core essence of the communist period for her: that one could not trust what the state told you, nor live in their world if you let yourself think critically.

* * *

When Diana graduated from high school in 1979, students with good results and a clean biography were automatically accepted to study English teaching at State University of Tirana Faculty of Foreign Language. For the three years of university, Diana lived with her family in Durres, commuting by train to Tirana for classes, and studying under the orange and lemon trees in her family garden. The three principles of university education were education, manufacturing work (*aksion*) and physical/military education (*zbor*) for one month every year. Diana's English language lecturers were Chinese and spoke no Albanian, so Diana graduated without speaking to a native English speaker, but she did acquire a repertoire of communist songs and slogans in Mandarin that she can still recite with "revolutionary tone."

Tirana students of Philology, Geography, History and Linguistics, and English, French, and Russian all went to *zbor* together in Mamurras on the river, just south of Laç. I asked Diana what happened at *zbor*, and she burst into laughter.

What have you asked me! Oh, the rifle was bigger than me! They lent you a uniform, but because I was so small, I had to take the uniform home and make it smaller, then I was ready. I had to go and say, "Soldier Keçi! Ready!" Oh, po po! But you had to go, and the officers really motivated you. I had very strange feelings during *zbor*, you know, I was READY to do it, ready to fight. An officer would come and say, "Look the enemy is coming from here! What kind of tactics and strategies will you use?" Everybody thought about it. "Ok! We will go in groups of two and three; we will go in groups of six and one!" We had a strategy because that's what we learned there. We learned the parts of the Kalashnikov and could reassemble it in two minutes. What strategies we had! If the enemy comes from this side, how are we going to get organised and beat him? All the imperialists and capitalists are losers — only socialists are winners. All these ideas were kind of stuck in my mind. I was filtering what they told us a little bit because of my family background, but there were others who had no filter at all, so they believed everything they were told. Anyway we all did what we were told, so everything was just, ummm, how to explain it... propaganda. They stuffed your mind with foam. Foam was put into your brain on *zbor*.

There was one toilet for 700 women. One toilet. ONE TOILET! You can't imagine – we washed in the river! So we went to *zbor* and we washed clothes in the river, and we washed for the boys as well! Because Albanian boys are not used to washing things! We girls washed in the cold water, and there was a *pasarella*, a narrow bridge, and we went up there as a group and we sang songs, nationalist socialist songs like war songs. "We will go to fight! Woo!" We had some fun, the training was OK, but living as a community was very good. We were young, and it was a beautiful story, singing together and being ready to fight. When I met American volunteers from the Peace Corp in Albania in the 1990s and heard about community projects. I was excited because this seemed like the community that we had before! But we had community life all the time; there was no option not to have it! We went to productive labour, to *aksion*, in our school groups.

We spent one month in Ksamil making terraces in the mountain sides, and a month in Lushnje doing agricultural labour, I built the railroad between Lezhe and Shkodra, I was a part of that! Yes! We did different things and felt part of making something new... but at *zbor* we had nothing to eat. We had a joke that we had to dive into the bean soup to find one bean because it was all water.

I asked Diana if that was a joke they told openly.

No! Just with your real friends! If you told a joke to your neighbour, or even just said something true out loud, such as, "Oh there are no potatoes in the market!" No! People were put in jail for that. But with friends, the circle had to be very narrow. At *zbor*, everyone was a friend, but only three or four were real friends. You had to be very careful in the big group because... anything could happen to you!
We were spied on all the time.

Student life at the university campuses also had a very active and central political force. The Youth Organization Committee (*Organizata e Rinise*) monitored students for signs of decadent Western imperialism in their dress and behaviour, in addition to examination of their performance in Political Education subjects such as Dialectical Materialism, Marxism–Leninism, Hegel's Dialectics, Marx and Engels' Theory of Imperialism, Socialist Realism, and History of the Labor Party.

Most Albanians, such as Diana, had one change of clothes, and beauty products were limited. There were no deodorants and only one kind of women's perfume; rose-fragranced and named 8 March Perfume after the annual Women's Day. The only moisturising cream was called *Shendet* (health), a heavy white cream that women used against nappy rash on children, often sticking to olive oil for their own skin. There was one kind of soap for the body (*Sapun Toaletti*), one for clothes (*Sapun Soda*), and Lux, a soap that came from abroad but could sometimes be found in the shops. It was the only soap that had an aroma. There was no eye shadow; students used a bit of shoe polish as mascara, and lipstick was blended into the cheeks as rouge. Condoms and contraceptive medication were illegal, and sanitary hygiene products such as tampons and pads were not available at all until the 1990s – women used cloth rags and soaked them for reuse, making *zbor* even more difficult if one was menstruating.

It was dangerous to stand out, as *fletë-rrufes*, denunciation posters, were in full force. *Fletë-rrufes* denounced individuals for their hairstyles, clothes or behaviour, and were posted in the streets, dormitories and universities where the person had been seen. A *fletë-rrufe* named the individual and their address or place of work or study, included their photograph or a caricature illustration, and detailed how they had violated ideological requirements. This public humiliation was an effective tool of control in Albanian society, where the concept of one's behaviour being publicly scrutinized to bring shame or honour to one's family was long established. Diana remembers *fletë-rrufes* at the university being issued for pants that were too flared, handbags, and make-up.

> The worst *fletë-rrufe* I ever saw was on a big flip chart. 'Very imperialist clothes,' it said. Picture, name and last name. This is the worst I saw. A neighbour across the street from our home in Durres, the daughter of a doctor, fell in love with a foreign sailor who came on a ship. I don't know what she did, but the *fletë-rrufe* said that she smoked cigarettes and wore different clothes. I don't know what she really did wrong, perhaps she was seen somewhere having a coffee with the foreigner. They put up a *fletë-rrufe* against her, then all the men and some women swore at her in the street, so she had no courage to go outside for a long time. She was 22 or 23 and tall and beautiful, and after I read the *fletë-rrufe* I didn't see her anymore. Just once I saw her and guys on the street were shouting that she was a whore and throwing tomatoes at her. After the regime fell, it became known that she had developed a mental illness, and I think the whole family left Albania.

At university there was a mix of people from everywhere in Albania. Foreign languages was a popular faculty, and many children of the communist leaders studied there. It was the first time that Diana met young people who lived in "the block," the cordoned off inner city area of Tirana where high ranking Party officials lived with their families. One could only enter the block with the written permission of someone who lived inside, or apply for entry at the ministry for a specific stated purpose. Most Albanians, therefore, didn't see the big houses and tree-lined avenues where their rulers lived until after the fall of the regime in 1991. Then there was a wave of domestic tourism as people walked up and down the streets, shocked by the modern houses with manicured lawns that were huge in comparison with how everyone else lived.

Diana first visited the block with a friend from university whose family were established Party members, their father having served as Minister of Defence before becoming the supervisor of Hoxha's personal security teams. At her own home in Durres, seven people shared two rooms, and Diana vividly remembers the first time she visited her friend's home in the block and saw how people lived in the Party heartland.

> When she invited us to her home, I saw a laundry for the first time. A laundry on its own, with a washing machine, dryer... I said "WHAT THE HELL IS THIS?" They had a room just to wash clothes, a room just to dine in, a kitchen to cook in, and a separate living room! "What the hell is this?" I said. Something changed inside me. "Excuse me?" I thought. "We have just onions and leeks in the shops! And they have fruit juice!" They had people who came and cooked for them – chefs! And they went to the diplomats' shop in Ambassador's Street and they could get everything there. They bought things with foreign currencies, not lek, and they often travelled to Italy and different countries. Then I started to think that compared to these people, we lived in real poverty. A whole room just for washing clothes when I had one jacket and one pair of pants!

The young people who lived in the block varied in their approaches to their wealth and privilege. Under constant surveillance, some understood the disparity in wealth because they themselves had been raised in "normal" families and later became Party functionaries or the wives of Party members, so they lent their clothes to their "normal" friends for special events. Diana had a close friend, the son of a psychologist, who gave a small circle of friends access to his collection of "yellow books," books that were illegal to read or own. They read the books that everyday Albanians would be imprisoned for reading: Freud, Kant, and Nietzsche. Diana described his house as "beautiful" and remembered that his grandmother in America sent money, and that they drank real coffee, which was rationed and hard to find for normal people, out of glass cups. Again, having a family member outside Albania was a serious problem for everyday Albanians, but not for the Party elite.

Diana observed that friendships between the normal students and the privileged Party students seemed to work as long as the non-block people didn't mention the stark discrepancy in wealth and what that highlighted about Albanian socialist society. She didn't confront her friends in the block about why her parents worked so hard yet never had foreign currency to buy fruit juice. When block students lent their non-block friends a dress for a party, it was always returned afterwards without questions, and yellow books and discussions about them were left in the block. "They saw that we were different, but they enjoyed their life there," Diana explained. The split between the reality of everyday inequality and the ideological rhetoric of equality became clearer to Diana.

* * *

One day in the spring of 1982 while Diana was at university, one of her father's colleagues came to their home with her father's watch, wallet and Party membership card. He simply said, "The Party wants him."

"From this we realized he had been taken by the Directorate of State Security, (*Drejtoria e Sigurimit të Shtetit*), the *Sigurimi*."

Over the next three months, Diana's mother asked colleagues, friends, and local police to help her find out what her husband had been arrested for, and where he was being held. One person told them that he would be released after a few days, others said that he would be charged with abuse of work and lack of vigilance for speaking about political ideas. Lack of vigilance was a criminal act, but speaking against the state was a political crime of agitation and propaganda, carrying a heavier prison term. It was clear to everyone involved that the arrest was due to inferred political dissidence rather than a criminal act, but the question upon which his life depended was the charge of the state. Diana's friends and colleagues distanced themselves from her, as everybody waited to see how association with the family would impact their own biographies. After three months the date of the trial was announced. It would be a public trial in the building of the Port Authority.

On the day of the trial, Diana's mother and brothers attended and sat inside the courtroom, while Diana and her sister awaited their return home. It was the first time Diana's mother had seen her husband since his arrest, and he was thin from the period of confinement, but able to defend himself against the charges of lack of vigilance at work and propaganda. There was a huge crowd of local onlookers spilling out into the street where loudspeakers broadcast the proceedings from inside. This was common for public trials. Diana's mother returned four hours later, trying to contain her terror and grief in front of the children. Sherif was sentenced to five years in prison for agitation and propaganda, a political crime.

Diana's mother couldn't just ask the police or the Party where her husband was imprisoned, she had to ask friends and relatives to use their networks to uncover his whereabouts and convey the information back to her. Diana's mother never asked who provided the inside information so as not to create problems for anyone, she simply prepared for visits. Sherif was first held in Tirana prison, where Diana visited him once, and then transferred to Zejmen Prison, in the Lezha area.

The immediate family now had a stain on their biography, and so Diana changed from having a good biography, to having a bad biography. This affected every sphere of her life. Her mother was moved from work in childcare to the hard labour of bagging flour at the local factory. Diana's friends with good biographies no longer invited her to their homes or joked with her. Diana's boyfriend broke up with her because he didn't want to compromise his own biography. Professors at university monitored her performance in ideological studies with more critical eyes.

I asked Diana how she herself felt about her father's arrest, considering her awareness of the regime's hypocrisy at that time. "I knew that it was true. Inside me, yes, it was true: my father had spoken against the regime. He believed he had the right to speak, as a person. And now we know this stuff about human rights, but during that time... I wasn't sure what to think. I had a very positive view of my father. I idealised him as a perfect person, someone able to survive in different systems because he was smart and he knew when to say 'Let it go, it's the Party.'"

Thus Diana understood that her father had broken the law by speaking against the government, and she didn't see this as a dissident action at the time, she was too young and raised in the system to understand what a dissident action was. To Diana's mind, her father had committed a crime by speaking against the state, although she knew he was right in his anti-state analysis. This reminded me of Thoma's explanation that the law groans when it is offended and it seeks to punish those who wound it. There could be no questions of moral justice or even honest criticism. There was only right or wrong in the eyes of the law, anything else was simply not applicable in Albanian socialist society; you were with the Party or an enemy of the people.

Diana suddenly learnt what it meant to be an outcast. One day soon after the trial a former school colleague approached her.

This girl had always got the best grades in primary school, but she had not been allowed to continue on to high school in Tirana. Her family had owned the tobacco factory in Durres, so they had been enemies of the people from the very beginning of the regime when the tobacco factory was nationalised. She came to me one day because now I was with a stain as she was, and she said 'Diana, how does it feel now?'

"Oh, it is very bad. It's awful!" I said.

"So you see how it is for us now?" she replied, and then I immediately said back to her, "But it's different for you, you are used to it! You were born with this! It happened to me just now!" And then I realized how much I wanted to push her away, that she touched something inside me when she asked how it felt, and I didn't want to be the same as her. Then we both cried and hugged each other. I can still feel her hands around me – oh, what humiliation I had put her through and I hadn't realised! I was so young, and I didn't know that the spirit of a person could be killed with just one word or gesture. Why shouldn't I remember this? It really happened, and if we don't learn from our mistakes then what happens to us as people? She taught me a big lesson that day, and I learned from her.

Diana still participated in the university curriculum and went to *aksion* with her class, and it was from there that she wrote to her father in prison telling him how her life had changed since his arrest. She told him how isolated she felt now that she was surrounded by people who were no longer friends and judged her according to the regime instead of who she was as a person. Her father replied, reassuring her that she was young, that there was a lot of living ahead, and that although it was painful it would make her a stronger person. Diana loved her father for this continuing close relationship, and she clearly knew that she was now living between the two worlds, one of naïve socialist happiness, and the other a reality of political persecution.

* * *

Just as the Party chose which high school and university course a person did or did not enter, the Party assigned teachers to their workplaces at the end of the course. There were regional Party priorities, but most important was that if you did not have Party connections they sent you far away from your family home. If you had a bad biography or were from an ethnic minority, you were sent to the most remote places. In order to thwart potential escapes, people from the seaside were sent to the mountains, and highlanders who couldn't swim were posted by the sea or by Pogradec Lake. There was no stated length of contract for these first postings, and individuals sought ways to move to places they wanted to be. Finding a marriage partner with Party connections, a good biography, or someone from the city one wished to live in was one way to achieve state re-allocation of work after a few years of service. As Diana said, "In that period the government decided what kind of food you could eat, what books you could read, what school you would go to. You were not able to make choices. Even marriage was not a choice. We have a saying in Albania, 'My life is not a choice; it is a solution.' It is a fact that we made solutions – we didn't choose."

Because of her bad biography, the Party sent Diana to teach at Avni Rustemi School in Kukës, a poor city on the northern border of Albania, a few kilometres from the Yugoslav border. Kukës is just 194 kilometres from Tirana, but the travel time in those days along the mountainous and poorly constructed roads took eight to nine hours. There were buses three times a week from Durres to Kukës, and teachers could only go home twice a year. Diana was in fact sent to work in *Kukës e Ri*, "new Kukës," a city constructed in the 1970s on the plateau 320 metres above where the original city of Kukës had stood since the sixteenth century. The original Kukës, picturesque and ancient, was submerged in 1976 for the construction of Lake Fierza, which dammed the two Drin Rivers. Residents of old Kukës were allocated apartments in the new concrete apartment blocks up on the plain, and they moved their possessions and then watched as the water slowly submerged their homes and lands. Surrounded on three sides by the new artificial lake, with the Gjallica mountain range looming in the east, *Kukës e Ri* was a new socialist city without mosques or churches, but was populated by those who remembered the cobblestone streets of old Kukës. The Party could drown a city, but they could not erase the memories of its inhabitants.

Diana was allocated a shared fourth-floor apartment with four other young women: two doctors, one veterinary physician and a chemistry teacher. They were all new to Kukës, and they were young and excited about living independently for the first time, regardless of their low salaries. They bought food and cooked together, and they had no television, so they discussed their work and gossiped about potential suitors. This was their youth, and they were all energetic and enthusiastic young women who loved socializing and talking about books, films, music and everyday life.

There wasn't always enough food to eat, and there were some weeks when only potatoes could be found in the market. Diana laughed a lot remembering how they had sat together around the aluminium-framed wood heating stove, the *kaftoor*, thinking of different ways to cook potatoes. The permanent availability of potatoes in Kukës was a positive thing for those sent there, especially since the Party had destroyed private gardens in the 1970s. Kukës was also one of the few places in Albania where walnuts could be found, the key ingredient for New Year and Bajram baklava. In other cities, women queued in vain to collect walnuts before New Year, and substituted crushed biscuits or other nuts for walnuts. The girls in Kukës pooled their individual quotas of 2 kg each of walnuts for New Year and then divided them according to each family's need as they prepared for their journeys home. Amongst the five women, Diana and Zana had experienced what it was like to be politically persecuted, and they were wary of criticising the regime in front of the others. They listened to Radio Free Europe at home despite the danger of denunciation, and the politically zealous one amongst them would turn it off in protest. Zana would shout at her and turn it back on, so it was a relief when the girls could separate into two apartments for the second year.

Diana and her friends discovered a new duplicity in everyday socialist life when they found out that colleagues at their various work places had extra-marital affairs, which they'd never imagined or discussed in university or with their families. Many people, not just Diana, spoke to me about how men in positions of power pressured women for sexual favours in return for food items or travel permits during the socialist period. Many people also told me about women they knew who had

View of New Kukës, 1986.

been sexually assaulted by men under threat of denunciation to the Party, and women who had refused sexual approaches from men and been politically persecuted as a result. From archival sources as well as oral histories it is clear that women lived with the threat of male sexual assault under socialism. It was not a threat in public space (as in the 1990s) but from within work and social structures. Public discourse in Albania since 1991, which remains dominated by men, has excluded these stories.

The teaching, however, was a joy for Diana. As with her colleagues, she spent hours at home preparing posters to educate the middle school students about literature and Albanian language. At school her senior colleagues monitored her work because of her biography, and she criticized herself at the weekly teacher meetings in order to show her dedication to the Party. The young teachers had to judge for themselves how to differentially treat students from politically persecuted families. Every school had unwritten rules regarding how to treat students with bad biographies, and teachers basically perpetuated the "class war" amongst children or faced denunciation for lack of vigilance. Children from families with "black" or bad biographies were spatially and socially segregated from the others; they could not win class awards or prizes, and they could not participate in certain celebrations for the Party. Some teachers did what small things they could outside the classroom to help the persecuted families. Diana strongly felt that children should not suffer because of politics, and she tried to be even-handed with all of the students.

The children from persecuted families in Diana's classes were distinctly poorer than the others, in what was an already impoverished region. Students often came to class without shoes, and had very little food to eat, sometimes just a piece of bread and half a pickled tomato for their lunch. The Romani Albanian and Egyptian Albanian ethnic minorities were also harshly discriminated against because of racist stereotypes, and Diana often remembered how her father had raised her to be aware of this racism against the Egyptians in her childhood in Durres.

Recounting numerous meetings she'd had with former students from those years in Kukës since the fall of communism, Diana said:

> When I came back to Kukës after 20 years, the guy who was the Director of Education was my former student, Ibsen. We were sitting at a big table – I said hello, and he stopped me and said, "Are you teacher Diana?"
> I said, "Who are you?"
> It was my former student Ibsen, and he said I was the only teacher in the school who fought for his right to have long hair. There was a big meeting. He said, "I heard you speak up for me. You said 'Why do you want Ibsen to cut his hair? He has his right to have the hair as long as he wants to.'" I said I didn't remember, and he said, "But you must! Because you also came to my house for my birthday!" I had forgotten, and I was surprised that children remember, but I had done it because I knew what it was like to be discriminated against for political reasons.

In 2008, Diana was reading an Albanian internet forum discussion about literature, when one participant wrote that the first yellow book he read was Remarque's 1936 novel *Three Comrades*, given to him in 1983 by his English teacher Diana, in Kukës. Diana was amazed that she had trusted some students enough to lend them illegal books, as the punishment for possessing, let alone distributing, these books would have been a prison sentence.

Teachers were expected to use shame and fear as a tool of the education they provided. If a student repeatedly underperformed at school, the best students in the class went with the teacher to the student's house. There they would confront the parents of the student, in front of everyone, about the child's poor grade.

> "I'm sorry, I will educate my son better," the parents would say. Then the student would stand up and cry and say, "Oh, I'm sorry, I won't do this again." These things were very tough, and these are the words that go to people's souls, when you are not treated tactfully, you are pulled up in front of everybody and the parents are humiliated.

Teachers were given a high status in the socialist hierarchy, and Teacher's Day was celebrated on March 7, the day before Women's Day. Students brought gifts to their teachers, and in such a poor school, the gifts were usually inexpensive or found items such as toothpaste, a cake of soap, a quince or a pomegranate. Diana and her young colleagues were touched by the sincerity of the simple gifts, and laughed a lot amongst themselves at the range of gifts students found to share with them.

Kukës provided one amazing bonus for teachers, the *tapa*. *Tapa* were the soles of shoes that had been thrown as rubbish into the Drin River in Yugoslavia, which then washed up on the edges of Fierza Lake. Children fished them out and traded the found soles to make pairs in the sizes that fit their family members and teachers. A pair of good *tapa* could then be taken to a shoemaker and made into a whole new pair of shoes, with fashionable low heels and of a much better quality than Albanian-made shoes. Children gave *tapa* to their teachers, and families and friends in other parts of Albania envied the shoes they made from these found soles. The river garbage also provided valuable materials such as plastic bottles, which were not produced in Albania and were useful in the kitchen. One woman who grew up in Kukës remembered a classmate whose brother found a small eye make-up kit washed up on the banks of the lake. She kept it to use on her wedding day, and was envied by all her friends.

Seeing first-hand what was found in the garbage flowing from Yugoslavia helped Diana further understand what her father had told her.

> Those shoes were testimony to what my father had said – that they had better shoes than us. They threw the shoes in the river and we got them and made better shoes from them! Yes, advertisements on Yugoslav television watched in secret also showed us that they had a much better life. Our government said we would build socialism with our own force, and that we would eat grass before asking the enemy for help. They said we would produce needles in Albania, tractors in Albania, but watching Yugoslav television we realized that no country can make everything on its own. Coca-Cola was not produced in Yugoslavia, but they had Coca-Cola, and then we took their discarded Coca-Cola cans and used them as ornaments in our homes! We sat them on the mantelpiece, or cut the top off and used them to hold things, or used them to make antennas for the television to pick up foreign stations.
>
> This was a time of change in myself. I saw the two worlds more clearly: this world, my everyday life, and the world of the Party. We were not living the best out of everyone in the world as the Party told us – how could this be the best life if we waited for shoes to float to us from Yugoslavia? If we didn't have Coca-Cola? Come on, we understood that Italian songs were beautiful and peaceful. When we sang Adriano Celentano's "24,000 Kisses" in secret, we saw this was not war coming out of capitalism! And so we began to really understand that what we were told was not true, but we couldn't do anything about it.

In Kukës, Diana met a good-looking, young physical education teacher from Tirana named Luan. Luan became one of a close-knit group of Diana's friends because he had a wonderful personality, being funny, smart, practical, witty and well mannered. Diana felt that he understood her very well and that they trusted each other. Luan played football for the Kukës city team and Diana and her friends would cheer him on from the balcony of her apartment when they played home games. They began to date, and when Luan proposed marriage, he also suggested they make the journey to visit her father in prison in Zejmen to ask for his blessing. Diana had already visited the Zejmen prison once with her mother, but with Luan they travelled there in the cold of winter. First they took the bus from Kukës to Lezha, and then they walked the 10 kilometres out of town to the land that prisoners were levelling and draining as forced labour. They filled their bags with rocks to weight themselves against the driving wind and rain. Diana had kept in touch with her father via letters, as the Party didn't allow regular leave time to visit in person. When they arrived, Diana was shocked by how old and stooped her father was, with his shaved head and prison clothes. Sharif bent to kiss Luan's hand in greeting and Luan stopped him. Holding Sharif's hand in his own, Luan embraced him. Luan's respect for Diana's father confirmed her belief that she was marrying someone who respected people as human beings, beyond Party lines.

In April 1985 Enver Hoxha died.

Zana came to me and said, "I'm going to tell you something and you're going to be happy." She was watching me, and she said, 'He is dead!"

"Who?" I asked, but ahhhhh! She couldn't say the name! She said, "He!" And I understood. Woohoo! Inside me I had some interesting feelings, dual feelings, I felt sorry for the person as a person, but regarding his death as a dictator I was very happy and I smiled.

I smiled because I knew something was happening – a new era, a new epoch for my country, for Albania, and for everyone, because he was a kind of block, the person that blocked our way, our dictator. I felt such relief inside me! I felt like a flower was blooming, or like a nightmare was gone and now I could think in bright lights – it was a very relaxing feeling. I felt something had just gone, but it was important!

The word spread so quickly! In five minutes, everybody knew, but they pretended they didn't. So the students knew, but the teachers didn't tell them anything, in case the rumour wasn't true – we didn't know! The students were 14 years old – they were not children – and you could see from their eyes there were students from some families who were persecuted, and they were so happy, they were smiling.

Regardless of the ambivalent feelings that individuals experienced when Hoxha died, everyone knew that they had to grieve appropriately in public. The school director watched Diana and asked her why she hadn't cried when she heard the news at school. Wasn't she sorry that he had died? Diana replied that she had been so sad that she hurried home and cried there with her friends. Over the days after the announcement of Hoxha's death on 15 April, the television showed footage of people queuing to pay their respects to Hoxha's body at the pyramid building in Tirana. Ismail Kadare, the famous Albanian writer and Party member, wept on television.

Ramiz Alia succeeded Enver Hoxha as the First Secretary of the Albanian Labor Party, ruling from 1985 until 1991. Diana's father was released in the amnesty Alia granted to some political prisoners in April 1985, and Diana and Luan married that summer, with her father present. "We were so happy," Diana said. "I remember my father crying with happiness, and I was crying too, and he said, 'You have been my friend and I thank you for not spying on me.'"

I asked Diana whether she was shocked that he had thanked her for not spying on him, but she explained that this had happened in many families. It was testimony to the strength of their immediate family, to a childhood spent playing music and singing together in addition to political discussions, that they had supported each other even after her father was imprisoned. If Diana had denounced her family, she might have saved her illusions of a benevolent state, her bright future in Tirana, her relationships with the children of privileged Party members, and she would have avoided relocation to faraway Kukës, but this was never an option for her.

* * *

In addition to the scarcity of food and the oppression of the regime, being young in the 1980s was difficult due to the severe social and medical restrictions on intimate relationships. Courtship was supposed to be chaste, living spaces were crowded, contraception and abortions were illegal, and engagements were long due to the difficulties of changing workplaces and finding a place to live. Couples in Kukës (and thus in other places too) strolled through fields or found empty barns and buildings in which to be alone. This brought its own problems, such as voyeurs who would follow couples to watch them, and bag snatchers who waited until the couples were distracted and then stole their belongings and ran away. Diana and her peers called the bag snatchers *turrsa*, and one could not report such a theft because it was unimaginable to admit you had been involved in sexual activity of any kind out of wedlock. Amongst themselves, the girls compared stories, but these events were taboo in any other social space.

Diana and Luan were engaged for more than a year before their wedding in 1985, and they supported each other through the dangers and stress of terminating a pregnancy conceived out of wedlock. The only contraception practised in that time was withdrawal, as condoms and the contraceptive pill were illegal. Pregnancies before marriage were frowned upon and children before marriage were scandalous. In addition, the economic situation in the early 1980s was at its worst, and hardly anyone, especially young people, had any savings. Finding herself pregnant when engaged, Diana asked her housemate and friend Tana, a doctor, to help her find a doctor who would perform an illegal abortion for her in the hospital.

Many women provoked abortions at home by inserting objects into the uterus themselves, such as knitting needles, sharp objects, herbs, medicine or poison, and neighbourhood women were often called to help care for women who were bleeding at home after attempting to terminate a pregnancy. Women from all over Albania told me stories about these home abortions, including the names of women who had died from haemorrhaging. In the hospital on the day that Tana told Diana to go, there was a long line of women in the waiting room. All were given the same operation: a scraping of their uterus without anaesthetic. First Diana was given a lot of pills to provoke bleeding, she didn't know what they were, and then the painful operation was performed. She was very fearful that she would die from the massive bleeding that followed. As abortions were illegal, and doctors helped women out of sympathy and at significant risk to themselves, patients were sent home immediately after the scraping to care for themselves through the fever and bleeding.

In the course of my research I also interviewed a doctor who performed illegal abortions in a hospital in Tirana. He was busy when I met him in his gynaecology office during consultation hours, but he had a calm and considerate manner. When he described how he had feared being discovered providing basic care for women, his voice became subdued and sad. Women were not anaesthetised, and if they died at home later, their deaths were not recorded in relation to childbirth or poverty, but as haemorrhaging or infection. There was no social or state recognition of the widespread medical problems that ensued from the illegality of contraception and lack of support for unmarried mothers.

After Diana and Luan moved to Tirana in 1986, the shortage of housing meant that they had moved into a small apartment with Luan's parents. Diana taught at a school in the village of Kraba. She left home every morning at 6.30 a.m. and took the local bus to the main road that led out of Tirana to Kraba village, on the road to Elbasan. Meeting her fellow teachers, they would eat pilaf and drink a coffee at the roadside bar while waiting for a truck or car to pass by *en route* to Kraba mine and give them a lift to the village turn off. Public transport and hitchhiking with state transport were the only modes of travel. From the drop off point it was a further 45-minute walk to the school. The Ministry of Education assigned the teachers a bus to transport them in 1986. In

1987 Diana finally fell pregnant again, overcoming serious problems resulting from the abortion of earlier years, and her son Rubin was born on 1 November 1987.

Diana was transferred to work at the university publishing house as a proof-reader and editor of texts in English, and she worked there until 1989 when she returned to teaching at Sami Frasheri School in central Tirana. Change was coming. In June 1991 the Albanian Labor Party renamed itself the Albanian Socialist Party, and discussed reforms with Ramiz Alia, Hoxha's successor. The students at Sami Frasheri School sensed the changes afoot and began to be defiant in new ways, but Diana and the other teachers were well aware that one could not know what the government would do next. There were no precedents for revolution or a thaw in the regime, but plenty for purges and accusations. Students provoked discussion by asking Diana if she knew who Michael Jackson and Mick Jagger were, signalling that they were finding information about the outside world and were not afraid to mention it. Diana would answer, "Yes! He sings every night at my neighbour's house." In this way she told the students, "I do know what you are talking about, in fact, I know even better than you. End of story!" In 1989 the students were allowed to perform Romeo and Juliet for the first time, which was taken as a political drama in the Albanian communist context of the time.

After months of increasing tension from meetings and student protests for democracy, ten thousand student protesters took to the street on 20 February 1991. Diana took her four-year-old son and joined them in Skenderbeg Square in the early afternoon. Surrounded by the armed forces with police snipers positioned in the buildings around the square, the crowds chanted "down with dictatorship!" and "freedom – democracy." A helicopter filmed the protesters as they pulled down the statue of Enver Hoxha. As Diana told me what happened that day, her eyes filled with tears.

> The policemen came with dogs, and we shouted "the police are with us!" I was present! We were in a crowd of people moving in the square, and some men stood blocking the road. The policemen

pushed close, we pulled back, then the policemen moved back, and we surged closer. It was a real protest, it was a real revolt, a real war, people shooting everywhere. I saw guys dying so close to me, very dangerous, dangerous, dangerous…

I felt like I had invented something! When we pulled that statue down we were so scared. You had to be scared because anything could happen! If you were caught and sent to prison what happens to your life? So I had the feeling that I was in a dark place and then something bright opened. We did it!

You know the feeling you have when there is something you are expecting and expecting and then you just do it? That's the feeling. We had been waiting in isolation for more than 40 years, and for me personally it had been 20 years of waiting for the truth! And then we got it. We got it in 1991.

* * *

Inspired by Diana, I set off to see Kukës. The new road made it a smooth journey of two and a half hours, and we drove past the turn offs to various prisons and places where people I knew had suffered: Burrel, Spaç, Kalimash. Arriving in Kukës, I oriented myself from Diana's descriptions. The school where she taught stood emptied for the summer with slogans written in blue (the colour of the Democratic Party) where red ones had been before. I could imagine Diana walking home from the market with Zana and some potatoes to cook for dinner. I saw the balcony from which the friends had watched Luan play football for Kukës.

I wanted to find the collection of the socialist period Museum of Kukës, so I visited the Cultural Centre on the square near the hospital. The women working there in the children's library were helpful and friendly, and then the male director of the centre arrived and took over. He wasn't quite sure what I was looking for, but he was eager to explain the history of Kukës and show me around. As he led me upstairs he proudly told me that his father had been an engineer in the construction of New Kukës. His father had been a communist, and now he was the director of this cultural centre run by the municipal council.

He led me to a door on the second floor. It was a small room into which the workers had thrown the building's many plaster busts of Enver Hoxha. Plaster Hoxha heads lay broken all over the floor, their podiums fallen askew in all directions. Hundreds of brown and red bound books with Hoxha's name embossed in gold on their broken spines lay open, face down, covered in the white dust of the broken busts.

On the next level the director opened a door to a much larger room. All the desks had been pushed to one side and covered in a huge mountain of photographs, which cascaded all over the floor. The director walked across them without hesitation to open a window and let in some air. The women from the library downstairs had followed us up and we all stood in the room, on the carpet of black and white photographs, together. The crumbling whitewashed walls and street dust blown through ill-fitting window panes had covered everything in the room with dust.

It is hard for a historian to stand on photographs, and I bent and picked some up to clear a space. I asked if I could stay and look through them for a while. The director replied, "Yes! Take as many photos as you want. What do we want these old things for?" and left the room. The librarians looked horrified and I reassured them that I wouldn't take any photos to Australia. I asked them to stay with me and we stood looking out the windows. The women began to tell me their stories.

They pointed out towards the lake, where old Kukës lay below the water, and told me that when the water level was low, the people from old Kukës gathered above the lake every night, hoping to see the walls of their family houses. They could make out the shapes of some of the hardier homes. Now some people seek compensation from the government for those properties that were taken, as do those whose family lands were taken for the site of New Kukës.

We returned our attention to the photographs. They dusted them with the backs of their hands, identifying the people in each photo by name. They knew everyone's names from their childhood visits to the museum with its handmade posters of communist partisan heroes, and from their lives in the small city. Not knowing anyone in the photographs, I dusted each one I picked up and identified out loud the activity the people were doing. There were photos of harvest time, planting time, of men at *zbor*, and students working with the community to stack the hay. There were photos of the funeral ritual conducted for Stalin in the street in 1953, and there were photos of old Kukës, picturesque and alive. Cats leapt from rock-piled walls in old Kukës, and women in traditional clothes, their heads covered in black-tasselled hats, leant laughing on wooden sticks and stared right back at the photographers. Men gathered outside the mosque to talk, and women and girls sat husking the corn together in family courtyards.

The women asked what had brought me to Kukës, and I said I'd met with a teacher called Diana. "Diana!" the women exclaimed, "But we know her! She was young here, a great teacher, and she married the sports teacher! Yes! She was our teacher but she was always so friendly. We were so young then! And how is Diana now? What is she doing now? Does she still laugh a lot?" We chatted a little, and they told me what they'd done – finished school, married, survived the years after "that time." Eventually we fell into silence. We dusted and sorted the photos as if we could put the past into some kind of order. After a long time the oldest of the women spoke. "Hajde," she said, "Let's drink a coffee together."

Chapter Five

Invisible Barriers - Liljana Majko

I returned to Tirana from Kukës to meet Eda's parents, who had also spent their lives as teachers, first in the mountainous north and then in the south of Albania. Eda and I both lived in Ali Demi, the neighbourhood beside the Lana river on the foothills of Mount Dajti. My apartment was in one of the new concrete towers, painted pastel pink, that swayed through the regular earthquakes, and Eda lived on the top (fifth) floor of a communist-period apartment block. Until the 1970s, Ali Demi was composed of single-storey houses with gardens and fruit trees. Slowly responding to the housing crisis, the Party paved Ali Demi Road and lined it with apartment blocks built of porous brick, lightly rendered in now crumbling concrete. There were no elevators or central heating, although these apartments were primarily allocated to families with members in the Party. Now these apartment blocks sag under the weight of the huge plastic water tanks that people installed on the roofs in the 1990s to solve the problem of water being available for only a few hours every day.

Eda's parents were visiting Tirana from their home in Delvina, Thoma's hometown also, in Southern Albania. Turning into the stairwell of Eda's apartment, I leapt the pools of water that leaked from a ground spring, and climbed the stairs, which broke off in fragments due to the inferior concrete used in their construction. Even these external stairwells were cleaned and decorated with rugs and rows of potted plants. At the fourth floor I paused for breath and to take in the view – the beautiful chaos of old Tirana homes below, only their tiled roofs visible from above, small terracotta islands surrounded by a leafy green ocean. This pocket of old Tirana was being encroached on all sides by brightly painted apartment blocks, and it is sad to know that the remaining gardens shaded with citrus trees and grape vines, built on thin and winding streets, will soon be destroyed by developers.

As usual, one of Eda's neighbours spoke to me in the staircase. Eda came out to greet me and pointed down to her grandmother Nure's house. Eda lived with her maternal grandmother here in Ali Demi throughout high school and university, and she often shared stories she'd heard from Nure about the times before she was born. When I met Nure myself, I asked her to tell me about her childhood in Albania during the 1930s under King Zog. Her personal brush with the monarchy was when the King's bridal motorcade passed by their family home and small shop on the Tirana–Durres road in 1938. Queen Geraldine had been a blur of white lace in the scarlet Mercedes-Benz 540K that Hitler had given them as a wedding gift.

Nure married Idi Shaqja in 1951, then moved to Tirana to live with her new husband and his family. She still lives in the home where she raised her five children and some of her grandchildren. Her daughter, Lili, married a man named Majko, and Eda is one of their three daughters. Selim Shaqja, Nure's father-in-law, was the head of the household, and he worked as a gardener at ambassadorial residences before and after the communists came to power.

I met Nure in Eda's apartment. She came up for lunch because Lili and Majko were visiting from their home in Delvina, where Thoma was born. They are a friendly and boisterous family, three generations of one family sharing an indefatigable and good-willed sense of humour and a commitment to making excellent jokes. I loved their dramatic ways of telling quotidian occurrences as comic sagas. In Lili and Majko's narrative of life together, being forced by the Party to live and work in a rural village, separated from their families and their children, takes central place. Telling the long story of their struggle to live together is a celebration of the primary importance of family in their lives.

Lili and Majko's love for and enjoyment of each other is evident in their constant banter. We discussed history, politics and social changes, but returned often to the touchstone story of their romance. Lili and Majko are unique in this book as Majko's family are Romani Albanians (from the Greek minority) and Lili's family are Egyptian Albanians, a group of Roma who identify themselves as distinct from Roma, their name indicating a community belief that they arrived in Albania in the sixteenth century via Egypt. These ethnic minorities have been considered separate to ethnic Albanians and have been discriminated against since they first arrived in the lands now called Albania. Under socialism, Romani and Egyptian ethnic minorities weren't persecuted politically as a class because socialism is the dictatorship of the proletariat regardless of gender and ethnicity. Nevertheless, racial discrimination against Romani and Egyptian Albanians continued through the socialist period. Lili and Majko's experiences highlight that even people with good biographies suffered as a result of persistent racial prejudice in the socialist period.

* * *

Liljana was born on 1 May 1954, and grew up with her four sisters and a brother in the house with a garden in Tirana. Her grandmother managed the household while her grandfather, a tall, thin man with muscles sculpted from labour, worked as a gardener at the home of the Minister of Education and Culture, Thoma Deliana, as well as for numerous foreign embassies. Lili's parents, Nure and Idi, worked in the Tirana coal-mines; her father as a welder, and her mother at the selection table, sorting the extracted minerals and rocks by hand. Nure also worked at home, shopping, cooking and cleaning for her five children. It was Lili's grandfather's connection with the Minister for Education and Culture that made a significant difference to the opportunities available to Lili and her siblings.

Working for a minister required security clearance to access "the block" where ministers and their families lived. Passing armed guards to get in and out of work every day, Selim found the minister, Thoma Deliana, and his wife, Virgjinia, friendly and interested in his life. A young man himself, born in 1924 in Elbasan, Deliana was one of the original communist converts who believed in universal education, including for ethnic Romani and Egyptian Albanians. Deliana gave Italian, French and English magazines to Selim for his grandchildren to read, and the foreigners at the international embassies where he gardened offered him suits and other second-hand clothes. He refused the clothes because his co-worker and neighbour were known to inform on anyone who committed the crime of accepting gifts from foreigners. Because the magazines were a valuable educational resource for learning English, they were kept hidden at home despite the fact that it was illegal to do so. Selim saw that the powerful people he worked for all spoke multiple languages, so he wanted his own grandchildren to learn foreign languages too.

Liljana attended the Mihal Grameno School in central Tirana until the eighth grade. Her grades were very good and the family culture was hard working and studious. They were not Party members, but the family was aware that life was better under socialist ideology for Egyptian Albanians because all workers were to be treated as equal. Albanians stereotyped Egyptian Albanians as more settled than Romani Albanians and therefore as useful as household help. Romani Albanians were known as tinsmiths, horse dealers and musicians. In this way, the dominant culture used stereotypes of ethnicity to create and perpetuate socio-economic segregation in a strict hierarchy – with ethnic Albanians at the top, and Romani and Egyptian communities considered the lowest level of society. Some Romani groups were peripatetic, and all Romani and Egyptian Albanians were considered an ethnic minority, as were the Aromans/Vlachs, despite the fact that many spoke only Albanian language. As in other European nation states, ethnic Albanians stereotyped Romani and Egyptian Albanians as inferior outsiders to the settled populations, even 400 years after their arrival. By 1945, however, Egyptians and most Romani Albanian communities were settled and stable, even if they travelled for work. Of course, stereotyping Romani people as unable to integrate into the community was a means of keeping them professionally segregated and underpaid as labourers, traders and musicians, benefitting the ruling classes. The social hierarchy built with ethnic stereotypes deemed the supposedly lower ethnic groups unworthy of education, just as it deemed women inferior using the hierarchy of binary gender. Albanian society maintained both the gendered and the ethnic hierarchy throughout the socialist period.

The socialist struggle for unity of the proletariat meant that race and ethnicity, for the first time, were explicitly rejected as a social order. While many Egyptians and Roma understood that they continued to be seen as the bottom of the social hierarchy, excluded by networks of pre-communist and communist power, they also understood that in the new system it was illegal to discriminate against a worker because they were Romani Albanians. To identify someone by an ethnic or racial term was considered ideologically offensive. Romani Albanian workers were to be treated the same way as every other worker, which meant unprecedented real changes in access to education, housing and professional work.

Attending school in Tirana with children of the communist elite, Lili experienced what life was like for those untouched by the punishing arm of the regime. She participated in the massive May Day parades that were filmed and broadcast all over Albania, just as Diana did. Holding her coloured square placards, one piece of the vast spectacle, Lili first rehearsed in her school group, then with ten other school groups, and finally, on the day of the parade, performed the entire routine in Martyrs of the Nation Boulevard, where Enver Hoxha watched from a grandstand in front of the Dajti Hotel. Children were given a red skirt, white shirt and a red pioneer scarf to wear on the day of the parade, which they returned after the performance.

In 1972 Thoma Deliana used his connections to enable the Majko family to buy a television, for which there were Party-controlled waiting lists in every district. Lili's family made their own metal antenna, as did everyone, and from Tirana they could pick up Italian television transmissions. The signals would be blocked whenever the Catholic Pope appeared, but it was a common event to watch the Vienna New Year's Concert. During 1972, the government intensified the "war against foreign cosmopolitan and bourgeois influence," and signal jammers were installed on the Palace of Culture in Skenderbeg Square, the centre of Tirana, and on the only building with fifteen storeys in Albania, the Tirana Hotel. Keeping foreign magazines in the house was illegal, but Tirana residents with televisions were able to see films from England, Yugoslavia, Egypt and Turkey deemed acceptable by censors until the purges of 1974 which imprisoned, amongst many others, the director of Albanian Radio and Television, Todi Lubonja. After this time, television programs became limited.

Thoma Deliana personally ensured Lili a place in the Foreign Languages High School. Her grades were high enough, but the school was primarily attended by children of important Party members such as the daughters of Fecor Shehu (Minister of the Interior) and Javer Malo (an ambassador to France and China) in Lili's cohort. The teacher of Party History at the school attempted to remove Lili as an unworthy student, until she realized that the Minister of Education himself had placed her there. This teacher may not have been discriminating solely on the basis of race and ethnicity, but it is worth mentioning that there were no Romani or Egyptian Albanian high ranking socialist Party members at any time between 1945 and 1991. The racist discrimination of the pre-socialist period was perpetuated throughout state infrastructure and society in the socialist period. There was no longer an explicit barrier to Romani Albanian children accessing primary school education, but without the help of someone in a powerful position they were not chosen by local Party committees to continue on to high school or university in the same numbers that non-Romani Albanians were chosen. The ethnic Albanians who constituted the socialist bureaucracy at every level considered Romani and Egyptian Albanians to be separate ethnic groups, and they were forced, overall, to remain an uneducated and poorer segregated community within the nation.

Lili specialized in English at the Foreign Languages High School. In the first two years, students did one day of military training each week, where they learnt military terminology, how to load and use a gun, and basic exercises. In the third and fourth years of high school, students did one month of *zbor*. Their high school class went to the village of Paskuqan for *zbor* in the summer, after the school year had finished, where they slept in dormitories like soldiers and did military training activities. The first month of the final two academic years was not for study, but for "manufacturing work" (*pune prodhuese*), and Lili worked in the Josif Pashko factory, making tiles and other ceramic products with her classmates. The work was repetitive and dull, and there was a common understanding amongst the students that such work was beneath the level that they would work at after graduation. Everyone knew to pretend that being a factory worker was an admirable occupation, even as they discussed amongst themselves the kinds of professional careers the Party might designate for them.

Lili was therefore familiar with the working world of socialist Albania, an understanding enhanced by visiting the house of Thoma Deliana with her grandfather on two occasions. She remembers showing their security permits to the guards at the entrance, and then walking through streets lined with trees, seeing grand and modern houses that did not exist anywhere else in the country. Her grandfather pointed out Enver Hoxha's house, although he had never seen Hoxha in person because the street was blocked and guarded from both ends so that no one could approach him or see him when he passed, even within "the block." They entered the minister's home by the small rear entrance for workers, and Lili was struck by the beauty of the double-storey villa's fireplace in a large kitchen.

Lili graduated from high school in 1973. All students with good biographies from the Foreign Languages High School were sent to university – the elite to continue English language studies in Tirana, and the remainder divided between Albanian language and literature, and history and geography. Thoma Deliana wanted to intervene and send Lili to study medicine with his son, but Lili had always been afraid of doctors, so she continued with the Party-designated course and entered the literature and language program at Elbasan University, which had opened in 1971.

In the photograph of Lili on the cover of this book, she is in her first year at university, standing proudly beside the car of the university director. The shiny curved metal of the car contrasts with the dirt that begins where the concrete university steps end. Lili casually rests one arm on the car bonnet, an open book propped before her, contextualising her proximity to both the car and the university, evoking the class mobility enabled by her higher education. With her thin coat buttoned high against the cold, Lili's expression is calm and amused, confident and safe. This same expression is common to other photos of Lili from these years, such as in the photo of her in a group of young women at *zbor*. Dressed in army uniforms that are too big for them, they pose with their legs outstretched and entangled, laughing. Cameras were not privately owned. State photographers worked in public space and gave you a receipt telling you where to pick up the photo a few days after it was taken.

Lili was the first of her family to attend university, and she enjoyed living in the student dormitory in Elbasan. The living conditions in the dormitories were rudimentary, but Lili felt an overwhelming ambience of fulfilment, security and hope. Students attended classes for approximately six hours a day (four lectures of 90 minutes per day) over three years.

Dormitories were segregated by sex, and students ate in the cafeteria. Six women lived in each narrow dormitory room, which contained one wardrobe, one small table and three double bunk beds. The rooms were approximately five metres long and four metres wide. There was no hot water available and showers were only intermittently functional, so the girls heated water by directly placing a heating element in a plastic bucket filled with water. The dormitory was crowded but safe, with the exception of the electrified elements heating the water. The women enjoyed living independently of their families and imagining their future careers, travelling to new places and meeting new people. Apart from parties organized by the university for national holidays and New Year, there were no parties or nightclubs, but there was enjoyment in being

Lili (centre) with her friends at *zbor*, early 1970s.

with the other students, and there were daily *xhiros*, the traditional Balkan afternoon promenades. Lili travelled home to Tirana each weekend to see her family, take a warm shower and wash her clothes.

As we learnt in Diana's story, university was structured around the three principles of education, manufacturing work and physical/military education. Students of teaching learnt that education was composed of content on one hand, and political education on the other. Knowing the basics of weaponry and military training from high school, Elbasan University *zbor* was one month each year in the mountain village of Kraste. There students marched every day and were evaluated on shooting, reconnaissance and military strategy. Lili was in the phone communication division. The student soldiers did their own cooking and cleaning, and the water was carried in jugs from the river. Students maintained the septic toilets themselves, and there was rarely a chance to wash.

From 1973 young people were under more political pressure than ever, and Enver Hoxha was determined to prevent any social or cultural liberalization. The fiercest purge began in December 1972 when the Party accused musicians in the 11th Song Festival of performing "degenerate music." In July 1973 the Party resolved to purge "internal and external enemies" in the leadership of the youth organizations of the Party. Students were expelled and exiled for "bourgeois revisionist behaviour" or for "showing a foreign face" if they were a young person with long hair, or dressed as the musicians had dressed in the 1972 festival. Eduard Rexhini, a current friend of Lili whom I met in Delvina, laughingly recalled that he updated his identification photo in summer 1973 to capture his cool new hairstyle, a tufted and gel-free cut with long sideburns that contrasted with the oiled quiffs of Hoxha and the old communist guard. When his father saw the haircut and photos that night he panicked – his son had documented the exact hairstyle just deemed Western, decadent and dangerous by the Party. Eduard shaved off his sideburns and hid the photos that night.

Between 1973 and 1975, eight ministers and 130 artists and intellectuals and their families were removed from their positions and executed, imprisoned, or exiled to work in regional Albania. Amongst the ministers sent to work in exile with their families were the Minister of Defence (Beqir Balluku), the Chairman of Central Planning (Abdyll Kellezi), the Minister of Industry and Mines (Koço Theodhosi) and Thoma Deliana.

On 1 May 1975, the Shaqja family was at home in Tirana watching the televised May Day parade and eating their holiday lunch together. After the parade the newsreader announced that Thoma Deliana and Kiço Ngjela (Minister of Trade) had conspired against the nation. Lili's grandfather almost fainted, and then began to shout and cry that it wasn't true, that Enver Hoxha had been seen visiting Deliana's house and that he was behind the false accusation. Lili's father, Idi, knew how dangerous

such an outburst could be, and bundled Selim into the other room,
warning him not to say any more or their family could be sent to prison
as well. Selim waited in silence until the next news at 8 p.m., and when
it was again announced that Deliana and Ngjela had been "unmasked,"
Lili remembers that he sat and cried like a baby.

The next day Selim went to the block to meet with Deliana's driver.
This driver had often brought Selim home, and had even delivered his
television when he had been allocated one for purchase. On this day,
however, he would not come near him. Finally, after four days of visiting
Deliana's house and asking the guard where Thoma and Virgjinia were,
a policeman told him to stop asking or he would "fall off the ladder
like they had." Selim came home and cried, and he never went back
to work again. He died in 1982 not knowing what had happened to his
friends, and only in 1990 did Thoma Deliana come back to Tirana from
the co-operative in Tepelene where he had worked in exile and under
supervision for 15 years.

The Shaqja family were more careful after this experience, but were
still never persecuted, or, as is commonly said, "no one put their eyes
on them," a reference to the superstition of the evil eye. Lili completed
her three-year degree in Elbasan and was sent for a year of practical
teacher training in order to graduate. All teachers that year were sent
to rural villages of the northern and eastern regions of Albania. Along
with three other young women, Lili was assigned to the region of Dibra,
and the small village of Shupenza, near the Macedonian border in the
north. Lili, Sava and Anila had studied together in Elbasan, and the
fourth, Salo, was from the Higher Institute of Pedagogy in Gjirokastër
that had also been established in 1971. On August 13 and 14, 1976, the
Hotel Turizmi in the city of Peshkopi was full of students waiting for their
new village assignments. Graduate doctors, engineers and teachers were
accommodated with ten people sharing every room, and the atmosphere
was electric with the excitement of young people travelling to their new
professions and futures.

The girls accompanied Salo to meet her classmates from Gjirokastër,
who had travelled by bus all the way from Saranda in the south to Tirana,

where they had stayed overnight, and then up to Peshkopia. The journey of approximately 450km had taken two days. One of the arriving students was a lanky young man named Majko Majko from the southern village of Dropull near the Greek border. His family had moved to the small city of Delvina, behind Saranda, when Majko was 14 years old, so that he could attend high school. Majko saw Lili and wasted no time greeting Salo and asking to be introduced to the girl who was always smiling. Over the next five days the directors of schools came to meet the teachers in training, and Majko made sure he was always wherever Lili was, telling her jokes and asking her questions about herself. On the sixth day, August 20, the students could return home, not needing to be in their new workplaces until the first of September. Lili travelled the western road to Tirana via Burrel, while Majko took the southern road home to Saranda.

Back in Tirana, Lili and her sisters speculated about what life might be like in Shupenza. Lili shared her special problem with her big sister Flutura. "Somebody is after me," she explained, expressing the specific anxiety of courtship in a family where one's parents had always chosen who their children married. Flutura asked where the suitor was from, and when Lili answered, she replied, "What do you want with someone from Delvina? Take your shoes off and throw them at his head! Tirana people only marry as far away as Durres!" Lili knew that her family had always said that they shouldn't marry anyone from further away than Durres, and also that her elder sister should, by tradition, be married first. To make a relationship with someone that would lead out of Tirana when others were trying to marry into the capital city was also an atypical situation. In addition, Majko's family had been Orthodox Christian, and Lili's mother was a secretly practising Muslim. A relationship between them would test both traditional values and the dominant logic of the time.

* * *

I set out to visit Lili and Majko in their home in Delvina to hear the story of their courtship first hand. Eda packed a bag of food for our trip, and we left with the dawn bus from Tirana, stopped for espresso and roadside meals of *pilaf* twice, and arrived in Delvina at 2 p.m. As with all cities in Albania, Delvina is an architectural mix of socialist-period apartment blocks, abandoned industrial buildings and newly constructed concrete houses. Vegetable gardens are carefully tended in the spaces between buildings, and those homes abandoned by residents who departed to other countries for work are either locked up and silent, or open, looted and used as playgrounds by the neighbourhood kids. The one-bedroom apartment where Lili and Majko have lived and raised their three daughters since 1989 is one of the few apartments still inhabited in their building. Many people from the southern villages and cities of Albania have moved to Greece for work.

On the morning after our arrival and welcome dinner, Lili opened the downstairs apartment, which she cleans and maintains for the owners who moved to Greece in 1992. The vacant apartment is exactly as it was when they left – a museum to the socialist period in that every item of furniture and decoration was produced in socialist Albania, down to the Drinos Liqueur, Durres cigarettes and Mimoza radio in the lounge room buffet. While men dominate the coffee shops and bars in Albania, women's spaces are the home. Here in this neighbouring apartment Lili fried *petulla*, small savoury doughnuts, for Eda and I. We ate them with fresh feta cheese or honey, boiled pots of sweet Turkish coffee, and talked all day.

Lili continued her story where we had left off, speaking about her first teaching position in the small village of Shupenza, in Albania's eastern mountains. There had been a lot to occupy her time. The young female teachers all slept in what they called the "teachers room" in the school. They pushed the desks together and put mattresses on top to make beds, their suitcases under the desks. The only heating was wood-burning stoves, and it was freezing, with heavy snowfall between October and March. They washed and hung out their clothes in the classroom where they slept. They liked their colleagues, including Avni Dema, Osman Patria and Hasa Manjani, as they were experienced teachers who had been sent to the rural area as political persecution. There were many students with bad biographies because their families were connected with

Delvina, 2012.

a large group of villagers who had tried to escape across the Macedonian border just two years earlier. Lili reckoned that it was the job of the secret police to control the people, and that she would just focus on teaching as best she could.

As Majko was from the south of Albania and was assigned to the village of Fushë Studio, which was 50km from Shupenza and high in the mountains, local people were suspicious of why he had been sent there. "They asked me what I had done wrong. 'What have you done to be sent here from there, where you eat wheat and lemon? What have you done?' I told them that the Party sent me there to teach their children, but they were suspicious. 'You have done something, that's why they sent you here,' they said in the beginning." Majko left his assigned village of Fushë Studio to visit Lili in Shupenza just two days into the semester. Lili was angry at his direct intrusion into her sphere, even as she was considering how much she liked this smiling young man. Her friends pointed out that although he was from the south, without Tirana connections, he had demonstrated something very important by gaining permission to travel to see her during work time – that he could form useful relationships with powerful people quickly. Majko regularly visited Lili in Shupenza, and when it came time for the New Year break, between 28 December and 12 January, he accompanied her back to Tirana, *en route* to his own family in the south.

There were very few vehicles in Albania so they hitchhiked a ride in a truck carrying fresh sheepskins. By the time they arrived in Tirana with Lili's heavy bags of apples, quince and walnuts from the north, they were tired and stank of rotting flesh from the sheep hides. Majko helped Lili carry the bags to her family's house and left her at the gate. When her grandmother opened the door and saw Lili with too many bags to carry alone, Lili explained that Majko had carried them for her and would return from his hotel the next day to greet them. Rested and washed, Majko came the following day and was quickly ushered into the house to meet Lili's grandmother, Nurie, while her grandfather worked outside in the yard. After Majko left, Selim came in and asked who had visited. Nurie explained the situation and Selim replied, "So let's fix it!" He thus gave permission to begin the formal marriage arrangement procedures, and Lili hurried to tell the good news to Majko, who'd been waiting around the corner.

An Albanian engagement and marriage usually involves negotiations and discussions about the ramifications of the match for the whole family. In the socialist period, one's personal and familial relationship with the Party was an important factor, in addition to the traditional issues of family connections, religion, ethnicity, class and culture. In July 1977 Lili and Majko both graduated, and the family engagement meeting for both sides was organized. Idi, Lili's father, was the only son of his parents, so he called his brothers-in-law from Durres to come to the meeting. By chance, however, Majko's father was called to *zbor* just before leaving to attend the Tirana meeting, and his mother couldn't travel alone or be at the meeting without him. Majko, who was away for five months of conscripted military training in the southern city of Permet, near the Greek border, decided he would still travel to Tirana alone. It was a shameful situation, but it couldn't be helped and his arrival alone would show that he had courage and was serious about the engagement. Normal people didn't have telephones until the 1990s, and so the Shaqja family in Tirana waited in vain for the Majkos to arrive. When they didn't turn up, they discussed the situation and concluded that Delvina was too far away for Lili to marry Majko. While the Shaqja family were at the train station returning to Durres, Majko arrived at the house alone.

With his head shaved for the military, thin and tanned from working in the sun, Majko shocked the Tirana family a little with his appearance, but Nure spoke up, "Well, where can we put him tonight?" Majko stayed with them at their home. In many ways it was lucky that he had missed the family meeting or it could have become a big argument; Lili and Majko were sure they wanted to marry for love, and neither wanted to elope. Majko left the next day, and a week later his father, mother and aunt visited. Lili waited for them at the train station holding a rose so that they could recognize her. Lili's father didn't have time to call the family in Durres to a meeting, and so when they hosted the Majkos in the living room, and Lili offered sweets, a vital part of the hosting ritual, Aunt Mako seized the moment. As she accepted Lili's offered sweet, she did not reply "thank you" or "cheers," but spoke the words used for those who are already engaged – *te trashegohet*, "may you have many descendants." This comment cemented the couple's future, and so Lili became the first person in her family to marry for love rather than through arrangement.

The formal engagement ceremony took place in June 1977 at Lili's home in Tirana. Everyone dressed up. Lili wore a new dress and sandals, and her sisters all curled their hair with cloth at home. At the happy event of an engagement, the bride offers sweets and Turkish delight, which guests cannot refuse. The families feasted together, with meat, risotto, salads and a cake with sugar syrup called *revani*. Majko's family presented Lili with an umbrella, a beautiful bag, a pair of shoes, fabric to make a suit, and a delicate silver wristwatch that she still has. Gold wedding bands could not be bought in that time unless one had them in the family already to pass down; many people didn't wear wedding rings.

Throughout the next months, Majko kept in contact with Lili through handwritten letters from his military training post. I brought up the subject of their courtship again that night when Majko was home from work. Over a feast of salads, seafood, vegetables and fresh fruits, Majko recounted his version of the story, laughing at how military training had constantly frustrated his romantic intentions. Lili brought out some of the love letters he wrote to her before their wedding, and we read them together.

Lili!

I am healthy and fine. I wish the same to you, that you are healthy and fine too!!

Today, on 5 September 1977, I received your precious letter, and I am happy that you are in Shupenza. I want to know: 1) Are our friends from last year there too? 2) Are you in the same room as last year? Please answer these questions in the next letter.

Here in Permet we are fine. Brief information about these last three days:

On Saturday: we had a dancing evening with the girls from the knitwear factory. We had a lot of fun. There was a lot of humour and jokes. This was the fourth night since the beginning of the military training. The Squad V, which I am part of, is connected with a youth organization of women from the knitwear factory with the aim to exchange experience between the two organizations. We have had this connection since July 10. We have almost similar working plans and objectives. The bureau gathers once a month and plans what we will do. What I say as secretary of the organization of Squad V is taken as the decision of the united collective. My friends have started to meet girls through the activity, while I ...... I have Lili!!

On Sunday: An aksion was scheduled in the work plan. We woke up at 5.30 a.m. to be in front of the knitwear factory by 6. But the dancing evening had made all my friends tired and it took about an hour to wake them up. As soon as I woke one up the others fell asleep again. In the end they all woke up, we ate some cold beans, and left. The sisters at the factory impatiently waited for us. We climbed into the truck and went to the work place, where we loaded stones. There were more jokes than work. The sisters had brought us petulla, bread with butter, and eggs. We enjoyed it. There were fig trees and grapes. The poor soldiers ate a lot. Groups of four (two boys and two girls) had to load water into the trucks. I could write a novel about just this one day, and I think that there will never be another aksion like this. Anyway I will keep you informed.

On Monday: military training. Only a few hours sleep, and now we have rehearsal. We are preparing a variety show number. So far, we are having fun. But I get upset from time to time, even a lot (sometimes for 10 minutes, sometimes for 20 minutes, and there are also cases of 2–3 hours) as I think of a little bird who is very far away. Mountains, fields and rivers divide us, with about 450km (Permet–Shupenze). To take the sadness away, I sing or start to do numbers that we here call "wild," and so I calm down. I don't know why I miss you – maybe it's because I haven't seen you for a long time or maybe because of the great love that we have for each other. I don't know how to express it. But, after all, in the end there remains only 23 days for us to wait, even though they feel like 23 months, they will pass and then we will be close again, close and together forever.

At my home everyone is well. They send you greetings. On Saturday, I will go home on leave. How is everyone at your home? Please give them my greetings, especially to Rita and Ada, without excluding the others.

Please try to find out where I have been stationed, in Fushë Studio or somewhere else. Please write me back as soon as possible about this!!

I kiss you with yearning from far away,
Majko Majko.

The wedding took place one year later in July 1978. Lili continued to work in Shupenza through the engagement period, moving into an apartment with the other teachers, and Majko continued teaching in Fushë Studio. Only married couples could request co-habitation, and so Majko spent time on weekends in Shupenza when he could. He became more aware of the difficulties of avoiding the dangerous elements of living with the state. One snowy winter night while walking home on the back streets of Fushë Studio from his compulsory ("voluntary") night shift manning the regional telephone office, Majko heard the sound of a man being beaten. In the crystal silence of the icy night, the voices were clear.

"We gave you this job to do and you haven't got the information. What have you been doing all this time?" said one man. Another man, puffing through pain, answered that he hadn't been able to enter the yard because of a tall fence and a dog. The other man asked why he hadn't poisoned the dog and continued punching him. Majko recognized the beaten man's voice as that of the village weaponry guard. Villagers had told him to be careful of him, but he hadn't really believed it. He began whistling to himself so that he couldn't hear anything more and so that they would hear him passing by. The next day, the guard who had been beaten approached Majko and said, "I was not who you thought you saw last night." After this, Majko understood that the Party operated in the village the same way it operated in the cities, and he was careful.

Majko and Lili celebrated their marriage in Tirana and Delvina so that friends in each location could attend, as is tradition. The immediate family travelled to both of the ceremonies. In Tirana, the families ate together in the evening, and then, after 9 p.m., 150 friends arrived, filling the house and garden with dancing. The orchestra played all night. In fine Albanian style, the entire neighbourhood celebrated a new marriage. Majko was the eldest of nine children, eight of whom were boys, and all the Majko family relatives and friends were invited to the wedding in Delvina.

When the bride arrives at the groom's home in Albanian weddings, the neighbourhood comes out to watch, and because Lili was a bride from Tirana, everyone was excited. There was another bride arriving in the street on the same day, and because Majko's mother was superstitious that two brides should not meet in the street, she had Lili approach the house from the back – a path that was through the undergrowth of the mountain foothills. She told the expectant crowd in front of the house to come back later when the bride was ready to be displayed, explaining that she didn't look so good having travelled all day and walked through bushes. Everyone laughs about this story still, as it captures the incongruity of old superstition in the modernizing culture of socialist Albania.

Lili and Majko returned to the school in the village of Fushë Studio to begin their married life. High in the mountains bordering Macedonia and the Shebenik Jaballnice National Park, winter lasted from October until May, with snowfalls as high as a man's chest. Students skied to school from neighbouring villages. Wolves preyed on the sheep kept near the villages, and the weather was unpredictable and difficult, so one parent accompanied the students to the top of the mountain from where they skied downhill into Fushë Studio alone. A male teacher accompanied them up the mountain again after school. There was only a primary school so "the class war was not severe," as Lili described it in the terminology of the time. Everyone in the village was equally poor and were all struggling to simply survive against the punishing weather conditions, so in the late 1970s there was no need for the Party to create internal hierarchies to prevent dissent.

Fushë Studio was (and still is) a poor mountainous village. Everyone worked in the co-operative growing potatoes and beans, and as winter was so long, people bought pickled cabbage, capsicum and tomatoes in the nearest city, Librazhd, or Tirana to supplement the dairy products they made at home from privately owned cows. Survival was possible because people had their own donkeys to carry wood for stove heaters and cows for milk, butter, buttermilk and cheese. Privately owned sheep and goats had been confiscated by the co-operative, but Party officials realized that if they followed the directives of Tirana and took the cows, people would die. Workers earned 100 lek a day and their wages could not buy enough food. Bread cost 50 lek a kilo, eggs 7 lek each, and meat between 70 and 140 lek. On a salary of 100 lek per day, people survived on a minimal diet. Local wedding parties served drinks and wrapped chocolates for visitors in celebration, as no one could afford to provide a meal. Teachers were more highly paid, receiving 250 lek a day, as were the directors of the co-operative and the economists, so they could always manage to buy food. Water had to be carried from a central village spring, so that washing clothes, bodies and bed linen was difficult. The children at school were hungry and poor with lice in their clothes and hair, which constantly spread to teachers as well.

As a married couple, Lili and Majko could apply to be housed together. First they were assigned the school physics laboratory, bringing the mattresses at night from a nearby house and sleeping on top of the tall desks and returning them every morning before class began. After a short time they were instructed to live in one room in the house of a local village couple with children. The man of the house worked as a night guard, and the morning after the first night spent in the house, Lili went to wash clothes at the spring with the other women. While she was away, the man returned from work and found Majko, at that stage just 24 years old, at the house with just his wife there. He flew into a rage and grabbed an axe, so Lili and Majko fled.

The Party next assigned them an abandoned room in the wheat storehouse. By this stage Lili was pregnant with their first child, and the chemical fertilizers in the storehouse caused her tongue to swell and made her ill. Nevertheless, the couple remained there until March, when Lili travelled to Tirana and gave birth to Marsela. Majko joined her for the summer break in June, and they spent the summer months with Lili's family in Tirana. Lili would have to return to work at the end of the summer. This was Hoxha's "emancipation of women," to demand that they be "free" to work outside the home, yet unable to choose not to work. Lili and Majko applied for a transfer to Tirana or Delvina in order to be closer to family and to have somewhere to live, but the Party refused their application.

When they returned to Fushë Studio for the next school year with the baby, they were housed in a room next to the bakery, above the cow pen. The smell of cow dung pervaded everything and they became used to living with huge rats attracted by the flour in the bakery. It was so damp that the baby, Marsela, suffered recurring ear infections and when she was just nine months old they decided to leave her with Lili's mother in Tirana to save her hearing. The Party gave Lili permission to travel to Tirana once a month to see her daughter. On the designated monthly visits, Lili hitchhiked from the village to Librazhd, and then took the train for five hours to Tirana. She could only stay for one day before returning again. The road out of Fushë Studio was kept clear of snow all year round due to the wood cut in the forests and transported to the Sharrat Factory in Librazhd, which enabled transport in and out of the highland village.

In the third year, Lili and Majko moved back to a room in the school and settled there. There were no toilets or showers inside, so the teachers brought water from the spring and washed and cooked in the room. They built toilets outside and used them along with the students. Other teachers lived in different rooms, but as a married couple Lili and Majko had a room to themselves. The Party still refused them permission to move to Tirana or Delvina, and they suffered not being able to see Marsela more than once a month.

In 1980, still living in a room in the school, Lili and Majko submitted their application to buy a television, wood-burning stove, and fridge, to the co-operative offices. As teachers with good biographies they were granted permission, and they used their salaries to buy the goods, which were expensive and beyond the means of the villagers who worked in the co-operative. The television arrived in December 1980, and the boys of the village came together to make a metal antenna and place it on top of the mountain, running a wire to the school in order to receive Tirana television signals from over the mountains. Without this antenna the village could only receive Macedonian broadcasts from Skopje. The entire village came to watch television that evening and many evenings after. When the 1 May parade from Tirana was screened, it was the first time that the old men and women of the village had seen it. Lili and Majko's room in the school became a kind of cultural centre and cinema.

The couple waited five long years until they were finally given

permission to move to Delvina, where they had their second child, my
friend Eda. As contraception was illegal during this time, many couples
discussed their options and co-operated to use natural family planning
methods. In Delvina, however, Lili and Majko were not assigned work
in the city, but yet again in the mountain villages some distance away.
They were also refused permission to build a small house or to take an
apartment, despite the law that they be provided with their own family
home after such a long time working separately from their own child
and families. Other teachers they knew who had returned from teaching
elsewhere were granted apartments for their families, and Lili and Majko
assumed that it was their lack of "connections" and their ethnicity that
played a role in the Party's decisions.

With no other option, Lili and Majko moved in with Majko's mother,
Seno, in their Delvina home. Majko was one of eight brothers and one
sister, and he alone had been chosen by the state to attend university
despite his siblings also wanting to continue with their education.
His father and grandfather worked as tinsmiths, and his mother and
grandmother worked at the *ferma*, the state enterprise. The family was
poor. Fifteen people slept in the two-bedroom home: Majko's parents,
his grandmother, his eight siblings and one sister-in-law plus her child,
and now Majko and Lili as well. Seven of these people worked in the
ferma, and four were still school students who did not work. Lili and
Majko earned the most, as teachers, and so while Lili could eat bread
with cheese, and sometimes an egg, the others ate bread with jam. Lili
felt bad, as there simply was not enough food, but because she was now
pregnant with Eda and travelling for six hours a day to work and back,
she accepted it.

While pregnant with Eda, Lili left home at 6 a.m. each day, walked
to the bus stop, took the bus for an hour, and then walked over the
mountains for two hours to reach the village of Dhrovjan, where she
taught from 9 a.m. until 2 p.m. She then walked the two hours back over
the mountain to the road and waited for the bus home. She would take
bread and cheese with her to eat in the morning, and then she would
eat again when she came back home at 5 p.m. As a favour, the director

of the agricultural high school where she worked let her eat breakfast and lunch at the cafeteria there before she travelled home to Delvina, and also allowed her to stay overnight in the school dormitory a night or two during the week. Until the final month of pregnancy, Lili also took part in "voluntary" labour, *aksions*, in the fields of Krane, as well as in military training, *zbor*, where she slept in wooden barracks with mattresses. All pregnant women were expected to not only work but to attend *aksion* and *zbor*.

Living conditions became much worse in the 1980s due to Enver Hoxha's long-standing policies of isolation and domestic mismanagement. In Delvina, as in Elbasan, Tirana, and other cities, people queued for hours for milk, which was rationed, and so could only be purchased with a ration card, called a *tollon*. Everybody received *tollons* for goods such as flour, oil, sugar, meat, and milk, but not everyone had the money to purchase the goods even if there was some left to buy when they reached the front of the queue. When Eda was born, Lili's mother-in-law queued for milk in Delvina, and Lili queued for milk in the village where she worked.

Because teachers earned a higher salary than agricultural and factory workers, Lili and Majko bought ration cards from poorer people, who then used the cash to buy enough non-rationed food, such as bread, to feed their families. Lili bought ration cards for beef from villagers for 190 lek for example, so that the villagers could afford to buy more basic food to eat and so that Lili could purchase meat. At some point in the 1980s no one could find soap anymore, and coffee, which was vital for hosting visitors to a home after a funeral, had become rationed and difficult to purchase a long time earlier.

The struggle to travel to work and find enough food for their children meant that Marsela stayed in Tirana with Lili's parents, and Eda stayed in Delvina with Majko's mother during the day while Lili continued working. One of Eda's memories of her mother from that time is waving goodbye to her as she left for work in a clean dress, only to have her return home 20 minutes later, her knees bloodied from where she had failed to find space on a crowded bus and had fallen onto the road. Lili simply changed out of her dirtied dress, and set out for work once again. There was no other option.

Lili and Majko had to be more careful of what was and was not against the Party line in Delvina, as many students had bad biographies due to their parents having fled to Greece. Teachers had to "draw the educative value" from every piece of information, which meant finding the socialist message in everything. A literary poem by Migjeni, who died in 1938, was thus analysed to be about how badly children lived under monarchism compared to the socialist period. School inspectors sat in on classes and graded teachers on their ideological precision and dedication.

Lili and Majko raised their children in a home filled with books, and they loved education. They bought the works of Enver Hoxha in order to know the line of the Party, and because not buying them could be interpreted as "ideological rebellion." When I asked if they had ever read or circulated banned books, Lili replied, "Why would I read a yellow book if not only me but my whole family would be punished?" Lili explained that spies became more prevalent throughout the 1980s as queues lengthened and people began to comment about the shortages in food. The common wisdom was that if one heard "there is no milk" whispered in the queue, it was most likely a spy provoking others to speak against the state to fulfil their own quotas of people to inform on. Spies were commonly referred to as "80 leks" or "120 leks," a reference to the amount they were rumoured to be paid as either part-time or full-time informers in Delvina.

School teachers interpreted all content through ideologically correct socialist lenses, and supervised the end of year academic competitions and political celebrations involving students on the celebration days. The celebrated days were 8 November (establishment of the Albanian Communist Party), 28 November (Albanian Independence Day), 11 January (Declaration of the Republic), 7–8 March (Teacher's Day, Women's Day, Mother's Day), 1 and 5 May (Labour Day and Martyr's Day) and 1 June (Children's Day). Lili and Majko did manufacturing work for 15 days each year, and every Monday they ran political information sessions for colleagues at the school. Every Tuesday they summarized the major articles from the newspapers of the week and presented this political information to a designated worker brigade. Party Secretaries noted in your characteristics file whether you had done these jobs correctly or not.

The pervasiveness of Party control over the decades not only isolated people from knowledge of the world outside Albania, but also eroded their trust in any outside information, as we saw from Diana's reaction to the *Voice of Albania* program broadcast from Washington, D.C. In Delvina in the 1980s, one could purchase a small metal box to place inside the television that enabled reception of foreign broadcasts. Televisions in Delvina region could pick up *The Bold and the Beautiful* every day in English being transmitted from Greece. Teachers left their classrooms to watch it together, and they made sense of the English and discussed what they saw. Lili and Majko explained that it was a dazzling and enticing view of a world that they had never seen before, but they also believed that this was simply capitalist propaganda. They saw that Albanian television also showed a glorified reality of what they experienced at the hands of the Party, and so they correctly surmised that capitalist regimes also showed an idealized version of society. Both Lili and Majko say, as did almost everyone else I spoke to, that they believed without a doubt that Albania was the best place to live in the world.

I asked Lili if she ever questioned the wisdom of the regime. "We were not against that system because we came from a system where we were discriminated against," she answered. "The government was good with us, they raised us, educated us. We had nothing before. In socialist times, we worked from the north to the south and nobody called us *Evgjit* or *Arrixhi* [pejorative ethnic names]. We were equal in work. Equal." Majko added, "Maybe they called us names behind our backs, or when we were joking, but not always with negative intent."

And yet Lili and Majko still become upset about the fact that they waited 11 years to be allocated a family home, and that so many years were spent far from their families. When I asked them why it had taken six years for the state to designate them an apartment in Delvina (which they still had to pay for themselves, in any case), they said that they didn't know. They both had clean political biographies and came from families with good biographies, and they worked hard and fulfilled their work requirements. Their families were poor and proletariat, but without close connections to the Communist Party (after 1975). I asked them whether being Roma and Egyptian was the reason for the discrimination and they said that they weren't sure. At every interview with teachers after meeting Lili and Majko, however, I asked what the standard amount of time to be left working in the countryside was, and the answer was always two–three years, never seven. On two occasions interviewees said that anyone left to work seven years in the countryside and then made to wait another six years for their own home must have either had a bad political biography. Or be Romani or Egyptian Albanians.

* * *

On my final day in Delvina, Eda, her mother and I went for a *xhiro* around the town. Children greeted Lili with deference, and everyone said hello. In front of the school where she teaches now, Lili posed with Eda for my camera, laughing as they copied the poses Lili had struck in the photographs of her youth. Lili's friends called out to us from balconies of apartments and houses, asking if her daughters were back from Tirana, and inviting us in for coffee. It was late summer and hosts served us sweet Turkish coffees with home-preserved fruits from their gardens. People shared stories of university life in the 1970s and marvelled at how the state of paranoia had given them a real sense of common struggle for the higher cause of national existence – something that was lost after 1990.

After numerous visits and a walking tour of the city, we stopped in a café for a cool drink. Lili ordered some fried potatoes to take home for Majko's dinner after work. The time passed quickly, and when we realized it was already late, we took the chips, paid, and left in a hurry. Out on the street, Lili flagged a passing car, and as it slowed and stopped we followed her lead, running to the car and jumping into the backseat. In the driver's seat I saw a boy of about 13 years, struggling to see over the dashboard. Eda and I looked at one another and both began to laugh.

"Do you have a licence?" I asked the boy. He turned around in his seat to answer me as we drove, "No, but I take the car to pick up my brothers." Then I noticed the two small kids sitting in the front seat beside him. Lili spoke in her authoritative and calm teaching voice. "He's my student and he's always been a good driver. Ten out of ten." Eda and I collapsed in hysterics and Lili laughed too – a teacher hitchhiking with her students and then grading them on it. He dropped us home safely and we waved goodbye as the old Mercedes lumbered away up the hill. We climbed the apartment stairs, puffing and laughing together. Majko was waiting for us on the last step, smoking a cigarette with a giant watermelon carefully leaning against his foot. We told the story of the student driver and he laughed as well, and then we spent another night in conversation about how life was "back then," in the recent past, in another world.

Chapter Six

Every Historian Has Their Past
- Professor Riza Hasa

At the end of a summer day of coffees and interviews with Thoma and Mevlude, I met a friend for dinner. He knew what my research was about, and I knew that he had grown up in a small village used to intern so-called enemies of the state, but I had never asked him directly about what he had experienced. On this night in particular I wanted nothing more than to enjoy a hot meal and a cold beer with friends, but as we ate he began to speak about Dragot, the village where his grandfather had been interned in the 1950s as a kulak.

He started to speak, stopped, said that he did not want to talk about that time, and then began to share an anecdote about village life before stopping again. I told him that I'd finished work for the day and that I didn't want people to share stories unless they wanted to, but he continued to speak. A major part of the problem is that while "everybody knows" that families were interned for generations, the mainstream popular examples, the discourses repeated on television and in print media, are almost exclusively the experiences of then-adolescent children of directly purged Party members who were in positions of state or social power, not the stories of everyday people. In the well-known public stories, a family that was accepted by the Party, that lived in "the block" and worked hard for "the people," is suddenly cast out of society. The social capital of these victims has travelled with them to exile and back again, and enables these survivors to speak about the injustices the Party committed against them. This is harder for those who were powerless at the time of their persecution and remain so now.

My friend was born after his grandfather had passed away, so he never heard him tell his own story of why he was labelled a kulak and *Ballist* and interned in Dragot. Yet as a child at school, four decades later, he was also treated as a class enemy. Approaching adolescence as the system crumbled into chaos, this generation experienced persecution in their formative years, but didn't have time to fully understand how the regime worked, let alone to find their own ways to act within it. They understood that those who were in power before 1991 regained power in the new capitalist system, and that the formerly politically persecuted were again widely stereotyped as taking more than they deserved if they demanded recognition or reparations. From this position, I could understand that my friend found it difficult to speak about a theme as broad as "life under communism."

"You need to speak to Professor Hasa. He knows about Dragot, he grew up there, and he is a historian like you," he suggested. And so, the next day I travelled to Elbasan by minibus and walked through the old walled castle district to A. Xhuvani University. When Eriada and I arrived, Professor Hasa was sitting at his crowded desk marking student papers, a cigarette burning in his ashtray on the windowsill. His was one of two small desks in a long office, with just enough space for us to pull up two chairs and sit at the table. The walls were lined with books about archaeology and Albanian history, and Professor Hasa began with a joke:

> Once, in that time, a teacher was telling her class about how beautiful and great a country Albania was. She was saying that Albania is the best country in the world, it has the happiest people in the world, that everything is in abundance, much more than everywhere else in the world, and so on, using superlatives. One

kid started crying and the teacher asked him, "Why are you crying?"

"I want to go to Albania!" he wailed.

We all laughed together. Moving between precise anecdotes and far-reaching analyses of the socialist period, Professor Hasa used jokes to illustrate the ambivalence and inexplicability of the complex world he spoke of. He had grown up in a family of good Party status and he had later studied history at the State University of Tirana and worked as a teacher in Dragot. He moved to Elbasan in the 1980s. Professor Hasa reflected on his own entangled position as both victim and perpetrator of everyday oppression under the regime. In our conversations he grappled with the impossibility of a clean-cut history of everyday life under communism, and he narrated his former self and actions as part of the bigger picture of political manipulation, where those who were oppressed were also forced to oppress others. Not only did he theoretically contextualise his personal experiences, but he constantly reflected on the self-censorship individuals developed to build lives for themselves within a terrorized society.

* * *

Professor Hasa's paternal family in Shkrapar fought for Albania in the Second World War, known as the War of National Liberation. German Nazi soldiers killed six men from his family in a massacre and only his father survived, severely wounded. After the war his father joined the Communist Party to work for the promise of land redistribution and to build an independent Albania. His class status was good, and the Party honoured those who had so many "martyrs for national liberation" in the family. Professor Hasa often cited Ismail Kadare's observation that Albanians welcomed dictatorship with songs and dances. He meant that some villagers did think that communism brought good things until (in his estimation) the mid-1960s, when the Albanian Cultural and Ideological Revolution began. In 1954, the Party moved his father and their family to the village of Dragot in the centre of the Dumre region in middle Albania, 40 km west of Elbasan.

Professor Hasa explained that Dragot was settled before 168 BCE, in the Illyrian period before Roman and Byzantine rule, and had thrived in the fertile region, hosting a large Orthodox Christian population in the eighteenth century. The Communist Party seized the lands and properties of local families who had lived there for generations (such as those with the family name Dragoti), and established a co-operative that grew wheat and tobacco. In the central plains, far from national frontiers and in need of agricultural labour, Dragot became an internment centre for the extended families of *deklasuar*, those people the Party accused of being bourgeois kulaks and whom the state "de-classed" to become supervised labourers. *Deklasuar* villagers in Dragot were seen by the state as enemies and potential saboteurs of the socialist project. Villagers with good biographies worked in the agricultural co-operative. Interned families, on the other hand, were put to work separately in the *ferma*, the state enterprise, manufacturing and packaging the wheat produced by the co-operative. Those who worked in the co-operative with good political standing were paid less than the interned workers in the *ferma*, although they had much greater freedom and access to state rights in everyday life. Such illogical contradictions perpetuated the segregation of "clean" and "stained" families across generations.

When the Hasa family moved to Dragot in 1954 they were placed in the home of a local village family. These villagers were moved from the comfortable upper levels of their own house to the ground floor, where livestock had been kept. This system of relocating trusted communists to share local homes was a deliberate Party move to confound and destroy the traditional socio-economic structures. Relocations made everyone feel that the new system had its own incomprehensible and dangerous logic. Trust was destroyed between families within a small village, between people and the state, and between people and the nascent idea that the government looked after their best interests. The government intended the forced movement of people to break networks of solidarity within regions, but this sudden movement also strengthened older stereotypes of regional and cultural identities, as the individuals thrown together tried to make sense of shifting community composition. People struggled to find ways to truly get along with new neighbours and form new communities, despite the division between those declared proletarian and those declared kulaks and class enemies. This was the intention of the Party – to force a reorganisation of Albanian social structure so that the Party was at the centre of all relations. The relationships between people remain tangled even now, decades later, as Professor Hasa showed by talking at length about the housing policies of the time.

> I was always worried because they put us to live in their houses. The Party forced them to take us in as if we were the best, as if we needed support instead of them… yet today they are good friends of mine. These political methods were copied from Yugoslavia and Russia. It was written in the constitution that "our state is a dictatorship of the proletariat." They said this instead of "don't speak because I will condemn you," and, combined with poverty, this shut people's mouths. If you are poor, your mouth just shuts up. To be seen as good by the regime you had to be from a poor village family, but this is quite strange – how can poverty be good? The people were suspicious of us, and they were right to be. But we got on well, as if we were family. There was no difference between us, it was politics that pitted us against each other. They are still good friends of mine because I grew up with them, but I always think about how they were removed from their houses so that we could move in. I was really young at the time, but I remember this. There was no big difference between us, we had the same problems. Nevertheless, there was a sort of separation, a sort of reaction, because we had occupied their house – it was quite natural. They were forced to treat you favourably, but then we grew up together. It was a fierce system.

To attend elementary school in the next village of Belsh, Professor Hasa walked a return trip of three hours through the undulating countryside every day. He loved school, and the Party allowed him to continue to middle school at the Pedagogic School of Elbasan. He wanted to study science and was disappointed at the Party's decision that he was to be a teacher, which was based on the Minister of Education's quotas in relation to the need for different professions across Albania. Nevertheless Professor Hasa enjoyed living in the dormitory with his peers in Elbasan, and he graduated at 17. He was appointed to return and teach in Dragot where he worked for five years before the Party allowed him to study history at the University of Tirana.

As a young teacher who had just graduated from high school, Professor Hasa was selected to be the headmaster at the school in Dragot. Sitting in his university office in 2010, he shook his head with embarrassment to remember that with the inexperience and confidence of youth he had thought the promotion reflected his intelligence, rather than the political machinations of the Party. As with many Party decisions, it is unclear whether they trusted him or hoped for his downfall at that time, but his confidence in his work meant that he continued to meet with people who were interned in the village and those who spoke out against the state.

> There was a carpenter in the village who I loved very much because he was smart, and brave too. Once he asked me, "How much is your salary?" I told him. He paused for a moment and then said, "Do you know how you are? You are just like dogs."
> "Dogs?" I asked. "How is that?"
> "Because you get paid to bark. The more money you make, the more you must be barking."
> I would always meet him. He is no longer alive. His sons were communists and they told me, "You'll get us in trouble – don't visit our father anymore." They knew what kind of conversations their father and I had. I liked him a lot because he didn't like the Party at all. He didn't like it and he said so. He was an old villager and he would play with words, for example, he would call the co-operative *gropative* [a *gropa* is hole, so a *gropative* would be an organization that digs people's graves]. He called the *shtet*, the government, the

pushtet. A *pusht* is a crook or a womanizer. He was a very smart man and I laughed because I was so young. But his sons were afraid. They were communists and people were frightened. In Albania, the state secret police, the *Sigurimi*, were similar to the one in Romania; if they put their eye on you, it was sure that you would be forced to become one of them or be punished.

The Albanians also use the expression that the walls have ears, and in the very first meeting Professor Hasa told us some jokes that warned against speaking freely, even to friends:

> Two people were talking to each other at home, complaining what a hard life it was, that there was no cheese to buy and that the rest of the world was more advanced. What could they do to survive? The following day, one of them was arrested and sent to prison. They told him, "Last night you said a lot of false things against the state!" But he denied it because he trusted his friend and didn't believe he would inform on him.
> "Yes, you did," the interrogator said.
> "No, I didn't" he replied, and so on, until they brought him the witness, the friend he had spoken with. As soon as the arrested man saw his friend he exclaimed, "Bravo! I was going to turn you in, but you were quicker than me. You could have been me now, but you were the quicker one."

In return I told the joke that Mevlude had told me about a man who went up into the mountains with his donkey to collect wood. To drive his donkey up the steep slope he whipped him and cursed in frustration. "Damn this life that I am walking so far to get wood to heat my house!" The next day the police arrested him for agitation and propaganda and the man under arrest exclaimed, "Wow! I knew you had informers everywhere, but even my donkey works for you?"

Professor Hasa replied with another joke – this one was about a man who was sent to prison because he had written too many denunciation letters. As the man entered the cell, the guard asked him if there was anything that he wanted, and the man asked for a pen and paper. This was an interesting choice of joke for Professor Hasa to tell. At the expense of informers, the listener revels in the image of someone vengeful getting a taste of his own medicine. This informer doesn't see that his ideological devotion is useless to the state, that even engaging with the Party on their terms (denunciation) will not make him safe. This joke lays bare the terrible truth of life under the regime, that there was no one to call on for help. The joke also presents the most popular answer Albanians have to the question of why informers informed: because it was all that *could* be done to show both subservience and distress in the socialist state.

These jokes could have conceivably functioned as a mark of friendship between people. In fact, the trauma of constant state surveillance and the high number of paid informers, combined with the punishment for joke-telling of eight years imprisonment under Article 55 of the Penal Code, meant that jokes were very rarely told, even between friends and in the family.[7] At the end of our first conversation, I asked Professor Hasa why he knew more jokes than anyone else I had ever spoken to. Was it that certain internment villages had a greater capacity or tolerance for joke telling? Looking sad and still smiling, he shyly replied, "Oh no Shannon, most of these were thought up after the change. Some I even thought up myself and haven't heard told anywhere else!"

Then we all laughed. I laughed because this act of retrospective rebellion sparkles and exhilarates, because any sign of soulful survival and engagement with the past is testimony to the resilience of people. These jokes articulate the incongruence between stated and experienced reality and the powerlessness of individuals. And today, each of these jokes and every response is a protest against leaving the inexplicable unspoken. "Oh!" Professor Hasa exclaimed, pointing to the other side of the room. He positioned his burning cigarette on the edge of the

7 Under Article 55 of the Penal Code, entitled 'Fascist, Anti-Democratic, Religious, War- mongering and Antisocialist Agitation and Propaganda,' one could receive a minimum eight year jail term for making a comment or joke interpreted as anti-socialist, or a maximum wartime sentence of 25 years prison or death.

ashtray and we moved our chairs out of the narrow pathway for him to
pass. Bending to a low cupboard under the bookshelf, Professor Hasa
took something with both hands, and when he turned around we saw
that he was holding a human skull.

"You see this?" We nodded, and I glanced at Eriada, who looked as
shocked as I felt.

"This is a human skull," he said, unnecessarily. "Recently graves have
been found, graves where intellectual people, innocent people, were
killed, and I was personally revolted to see that the bones of these people
were put in the plastic bags used for bins, and when they were reburied,
they were thrown into the ground like rubbish. I was revolted. When
I saw that on TV, it felt like they were being killed a second time. They
should be treated with respect! I am an archaeologist. When I discover a
2,000-year-old grave, I treat it with respect because it is a human being,
and it is 1,000 or 2,000 years old. Some time ago, I was digging for work,
and I found the cemetery of a church that I thought could be medieval.
There I very carefully uncovered this human skull. I believe that it is from
the thirteenth or fourteenth century. As far as I can tell, it is a female
skull. I might send it to Italy to have it analysed for its age. I mean, even
this is treated with a lot of care, a lot of care and respect, what about
those others? I've published articles about this in a newspaper, and the
former politically persecuted know of my work, but the state doesn't do
anything."

He placed the skull back in the cupboard and closed the door, lamenting
the refusal of the state to take care of the human remains when mass
graves of the socialist period are uncovered.

* * *

As a child, Professor Hasa heard criticism of the socialist regime close
to home. His mother's brother had studied engineering in St Petersburg,
and he and his friends in their homes in Tirana referred to Enver Hoxha,
as Thoma did amongst friends, as "the king." When the young Professor

Hasa asked his uncle why there was nothing authored by Enver Hoxha in his bookshelves, he showed him Tito's text entitled *Methods of the Yugoslav Communists* and said that this was the only book one needed to understand Hoxha. When Professor Hasa asked him how the world was outside Albania, his uncle mysteriously ended the conversation with the statement, "You would not understand even if I told you."

When Professor Hasa began his four years of study at the State University of Tirana, he easily settled into dormitory life and enjoyed the city. He was a dedicated and successful student, twice listed in the table of merits for his outstanding results. In our interviews, Professor Hasa stressed that he could not help but fondly remember this period because it was his youth, regardless of the oppression, yet he spoke with some regret about this time.

> Most of that time I used my reason more than my passion. And this can kill a person inside. On the other hand, student life was beautiful, as everywhere in the world. All those special activities! Those days when we "volunteered" to build railways and seed the hills with trees were beautiful because we felt we were working for something bigger, for our country, and that gave us honour. But it was a fact that no one dared to speak their mind or to say aloud what they really believed.
>
> Life in the dorms was just a simple life, but we learned a lot from the foreign students who stayed there. A Vietnamese exchange student told me that Vietnamese students who had "friends" went to big countries to study, but those without connections came to Albania. Sometimes when we went out on *aksions*, other Marxist–Leninist groups from the West came and preached to us about how good Albanian communism was. We believed them, of course, because we didn't know anything about other countries – we didn't know that for them it was just a paid vacation in Albania. In my final years at university in the late 1970s, televisions appeared in the dormitories, one per floor, and no foreign channels were allowed. But I started to ask questions. Why do the Party members go to

the West when they are sick? Why do they send their children
to study there?

Students in the dormitories were provided with cafeteria food which
they found good. From the monthly stipend of 3,000 lek, Professor Hasa
needed around 2,400 lek for living expenses and was able to save 500 lek
to buy vital new clothes or books. The majority of students owned just
one set of clothes, and individuals were thus recognizable by a description
of what they wore every day. Just as Diana was described as wearing a
red coat, Professor Hasa at this time wore a pair of brown trousers that
were baggy at the beginning of his student life, and gradually grew tighter
around the top from the regular cafeteria meals. Students sought out
tailors who could make or modify clothes for them, and Professor Hasa's
tailor was a woman in the building called "Pallati Armeneve" near the
Philology Faculty. He would watch the building until there was no one
coming or going, then visit her so that she could do the black market
tailoring work in addition to her state-registered work. In the summer
break, students who were not from privileged or urban backgrounds
returned to their villages to earn money doing agricultural work so that
they could afford the books and clothes for their next academic year.
There was no chance to take a vacation.

After 1973 the communist youth organizations on campuses
monitored the "moral standards" of students more severely due to the
Party's declared "war against liberalism." In this new wave of "vigilance
against bourgeois revisionism," there were no published lists of what
behaviour or dress actually constituted a revisionist threat, so the students
were often unsure of what styles would be denounced. This put the
burden of policing onto the community, making self-censorship vital
to survival. Life in this time became harder in terms of male–female
relations, as a couple seen having a coffee in public together risked
being pressured to marry, and sexual relations were limited not only by
tradition, but also by the fact that contraceptive pills and condoms were
unknown and abortions were illegal.

At Tirana University, *fletë-rrufes* were posted in the hallways and dormitories, denouncing individuals by name for their hairstyles, clothes or behaviour. In one case, Professor Hasa was part of a delegation to the Higher Institute of Agriculture outside of Tirana, a campus reputed to have such a high number of *fletë-rrufes* that they covered the corridor walls of all five floors of the building. At one meeting between the youth groups of the two campuses, one of the students mentioned that Professor Hasa had very modern hair. It was longer than he usually wore it, and he fled the meeting in fear of being publicly denounced.

One could not hope to get away with silence, however, as students had to put forward serious denunciations in youth meetings or risk being denounced themselves as lacking enthusiasm and commitment. Students could raise their chances of academic success through gaining Party merit with energetic participation. Professor Hasa remembered one occasion when he was obliged to make a criticism in a meeting of Party youth, and he chose to denounce a friend whose father was a professor, calculating that her position was safer than others, for "showing liberal attitudes." She denied it was so, and criticised him in return for "wearing cowboy fashion." He had no idea what this meant, but as he had gained weight through eating regular meals at the cafeteria and had his pants let out at the waist, he reckoned it was a criticism of his expanding (but still narrow) waistline. When he shared this interpretation with a small group of trusted friends later, everyone laughed. His tailor had let out the legs of his pants so that they appeared more bell-bottomed than usual. He simply hadn't known the cultural reference to American fashion and "cowboys" in order to understand the accusation. Ironically, one needed to access a certain level of "decadent, bourgeois" cultural capital in order to successfully denounce others and survive. In the culture of public denunciation, there was a fine line between self-criticism and self-defence, which was vital to advancement in the system.

Denunciations in meetings were not the only political hurdle for students; anonymous denunciations were also common and taken seriously by the Party administrators within the University. Professor Hasa was denounced in an anonymous letter in his penultimate year at university. The same friend he had criticized, the professor's daughter, told him that as Youth Secretary of the Party on campus she had heard about the letter. Professor Hasa went to the university secretariat in terror, knowing that one letter could lead to his expulsion, but the secretary asked him, "Did you hear about the letter from us?" By this she meant that if the existence of a letter had not been communicated to him directly, then a letter did not exist for him to know about and was not a subject they could discuss. Over the next days of intense stress, however, numerous teachers gave him signs that they were supportive of his esteemed place in their classes, and from this he deduced that the accusations had been refuted inside the University Party Committee meetings. In this system there was no such thing as straightforward and clear rules for behaviour or for punishment; one denunciation could condemn you to a life of labour in a far-flung village.

Later that year, in a submission signed by teachers and student delegates at the university, Professor Hasa was invited to join the Party. This was not an invitation to be taken for granted, as teachers such as Liljana worked their whole lives for the Party and were never invited to join. Professor Hasa believes he was invited because he was an involved student delegate, achieved high study results, took part in voluntary work programs, and had a good biography and a reputable family that included Party members. He was also male and was not from an ethnic minority; ethnic Albanian men dominated Party ranks. The dilemma was to understand how much the local Party committee knew about him and his family already, and what their information contained. There was a risk that accepting membership would invite close scrutiny, and scrutiny was dangerous.

Professor Hasa wrote a letter to the Party at the university saying that he felt Party membership was too much of an honour for him at such an early stage and that he would rather wait and strive to earn it a bit later. With great relief, time passed without anyone taking close interest in what lay behind his refusal and he finished his degree in good standing with the Party in order to be returned to a teaching position in Belsh, and then in Dragot.

The role of a teacher was to take the Party to the masses. When the teachers in Dragot drew up their lesson plans, they had to specify goals for the class, such as "to increase love for comrade Enver." Professor Hasa explained that if this wasn't written, "one could be accused of making a political mistake, and at the next Party meeting they would be asked why they hadn't written an intention to increase love for Enver and the Party in the lesson plan." Each classroom had a photograph of Enver Hoxha at the front, and school walls inside and out were painted with socialist slogans in red, such as

Pioneers! Read more books about Politics, Art and Science!

Other slogans were adapted from those written across apartment blocks, such as **Organisation! Discipline! Emulation!** The school curriculum was divided into the three categories of volunteer work, study, and ideology, and the language itself was dominated by words such as collective (rather than community), defence and vigilance. *Enver edhe Partia* (Enver and the Party) was such a common slogan on walls, newspapers, television and radio, that Professor Hasa's five-year-old niece once asked him if Partia was the name of Uncle Enver's wife.

The elementary school in Dragot had approximately 600 students in the 1980s, and roughly half were from *deklasuar* families interned in the village as political enemies of the state. These families were widely believed to have had higher cultural and educational standing than local villagers, having sometimes come from the cities, and supposedly the upper classes. Interned families are remembered today as having brought new culture to the villages; they grew flowers on balconies, were multilingual, and prioritised education. Many former teachers have told me that the most intelligent children in classes were often those from persecuted families, as they studied harder than others knowing they were under constant surveillance. It could also be, however, that there were simply so many families considered enemies of the state in Albania (statistics were not kept, but are believed to have been about 20% of the population) that they performed at the same level as non-persecuted children but stood out more to teachers because they had to exclude them from classroom activities.

As we have heard from Diana's stories of teaching in Kukës, teachers were not allowed to formally recognize the achievements of *deklasuar* students. Students with bad biographies were not allowed to receive the highest marks in the class regardless of their true ranking, and were usually prevented from going on to higher education or professional positions above the status of labourers. The majority of teachers I spoke to claimed to have attempted to informally redress the exclusion of children from persecuted families. In reality, however, children only came to understand in adulthood that they had been shown any small kindnesses in the overwhelming setting of constant discrimination. The injustices that teachers committed against students continue to pain both the targeted students and some of their former teachers.

Professor Hasa repeated stories in every interview about how teachers were forced to treat students. These stories were clearly very important to his memories of how he became complicit with the violence of the system, regardless of his personal support for these students. Knowing that the *deklasuar* students excelled at the Dragot school, he once instructed a teacher being supervised by an inspector to pre-warn the *deklasuar* students not to raise their hands even if they knew the answers. This way, the inspector could not accuse the teacher of succeeding only because the school had students from the enemy classes. A teacher had to be active in the class war, even and especially against the children of those deemed enemies of the state one or two generations earlier. This treatment scapegoated innocent children and re-created the *deklasuar*, stereotyped as superior in intelligence and culture, as a threat reborn in each generation.

Teachers often tried to protect students from punishment by making it clear that they should not overstep the invisible lines of exclusion. The case above is an example; both the *deklasuar* students and the teacher were safe in silence during inspections. Professor Hasa reflected on how his actions in that time had affected young people, which was not the case with one of his former colleagues who remained adamant in an interview that she had treated all students equally. Professor Hasa told me on multiple occasions that he had once caught a *deklasuar* pupil in his class named Teresa looking at colour photographs of her family, which she'd hidden in her school geography book. Teresa's family had migrated to America, and having a relationship with "traitors" in the West was heavily persecuted. When Professor Hasa saw the photos he didn't send her to the principal, but closed the book, knocked her head hard with his knuckle and said, "You must leave those things at home." Every time he told me about Teresa, Professor Hasa wondered where she was now, whether her head had hurt where he'd knocked her, and whether she had come to understand later why he'd reacted that way.

Professor Hasa also told a story of one day when photos of the outstanding students of the school were to be taken, and he called up all the students except for the one girl who was top of the class. She was *deklasuar*, and therefore could not have her picture in the top position. "I was the one who had not called her name, and her eyes burned with hurt," Professor Hasa said. When he repeated these stories, Professor Hasa spoke about the need for everyone who did something wrong in that period to "not be duplicitous anymore, but to be sincere and admit that they acted as humans do, and simply say openly what negative things they did and ask for forgiveness from those they hurt." This is an important point; as long as those who caused the most harm in that time remain in control of public discourse and deny their responsibility for wrongdoing, then the everyday people who feel guilty for their actions cannot easily apologise for the things they did.

Despite it being considered a dangerous activity for someone with a good biography, Professor Hasa spent time with families that were interned in Dragot for political reasons. His close friendship with the old carpenter was well known and people often saw them talking together. Despite the pervasive *Sigurimi* informant networks, there were some relationships of friendship and support between the persecuted and the precious few who dared to associate with them, providing either material help or moral support through clandestine social contact. Professor Hasa, as with the other people in this book, knew who spied on him and on others by the questions they asked and by signs of unusually invasive curiosity. Everyone also knew that their work supervisors kept detailed characteristics files about each employee. This was well known, even though the content was for Party eyes only, because everyone, especially those with good biographies, was asked sooner or later to contribute to the characteristics files of others. In Dragot and Elbasan, as in other places in Albania, some of the most notorious prosecutors, torturers and spies were socially excluded, assaulted and even murdered after 1991.

In Professor Hasa's worldview, there was a spectrum of people and behaviours. Some people followed orders but treated people with respect and avoided extra cruelty, while others were "more communist than Enver," taking orders to extremes of persecution and destruction. One example of this was the demolition of Dragot's Saint Mary Christian Orthodox Church, which had stood since the eighteenth century and was famous for its murals. It had been spared desecration or attack in the 1967 move to atheism, when the Party decided to preserve it as a cultural monument to extinct religion. It was one Party member alone who took it upon himself to smash and destroy the building with a pick and shovel in 1968.

Professor Hasa was unusual in his determination to discuss past wrongs in order to see how they could be made right, an interest that made sense considering his intelligence and disappointment with the "transition period" of politics and society since 1992. In meetings with his former students, Professor Hasa seized the chance to openly discuss the negative experiences of social exclusion with them, and it is clear that he is not simply of the opinion that he was forced to persecute the students and is thus blameless. Rather, he perceives his own actions as those that enabled the agenda of the state. In this return to the question of individual agency in the traumatic events of the recent past, Professor Hasa exercised a radical sincerity and took responsibility for his role in the history of the regime in everyday life. It was in this spirit that Professor Hasa suggested we visit Dragot, and I accepted.

Chapter Seven

Day Trip to Dragot

The Dumre region in central Albania is a fertile crescent of agricultural land south of Tirana and west of Elbasan. Professor Hasa and I set out early to travel the 40 km from Elbasan to the village of Dragot, in Dumre, on a cloudy spring day. Our route would take us south-west from Elbasan, through Cërrik and Belsh. Originally forested and known for its undulating hills and 85 lakes, the Party focused on agricultural production of all kinds of fruit, grains and tobacco in the local co-operatives and state enterprises (*ferma*) of Dumre.

I had met a lot of people who had been forced to live in the region because they or their ancestors had been categorised as political enemies, but that could be said of the whole of central Albania. Perhaps the Dumre region struck me as a particularly common place for internment because in addition to friends, I had interviewed numerous midwives who worked there in the 1980s. The midwife of Dragot delivered 220 babies each year to the population that she described as mostly politically persecuted families. The Party had also built the biggest prison for women in Dumre, first at Qyteti Stalin, and then, after 1978, in the village of Kosovë. One of my good friends had been a prisoner in Kosovë, and had been forced to labour in Dragot, about five kilometres across the fields. I was excited and nervous about the day trip with Professor Hasa, unsure of how it would feel to carry the memories of people I loved into the physical places where they had suffered so much.

The potholes in the asphalted road grew wider and deeper as we drove through Cërrik and stopped for the first cigarette break on the other side of the village. The low grey clouds misted us with rain as we surveyed the 16 Chinese short-wave radio transmission towers; the old steel towers stretched across the green valley, the mountains of Berat were the hazy blue horizon. From 1967, these towers transmitted Radio Tirana on short-wave radio to the rest of the world, including programs in foreign languages. Foreigners who moved to Tirana to support Hoxha's regime recited the Party's daily scripts on air in their native languages, hoping to make the world a better place by sharing the Albanian Party line.

As we drove on, we stopped for any oncoming traffic in order to negotiate the single lane and avoid the deep irrigation canals on both sides. Professor Hasa pointed out the fields used for *zbor*, and spoke about one activity amongst many that he'd been part of, where two sides had had to act out a battle in which a soldier would pretend to be killed. They'd chosen the smallest man in the group to play the designated victim, in consideration of the hill they would climb with his dead weight. After they played out the entire scuffle, they carried the "dead" soldier up the hill, dug his grave, and made a speech in honour of his sacrifice of life for Albania's freedom. The soldier happened to be Roma, and at his burial speech the speaker used pejorative language when he said, "He is a black *Jevg* who gave his life for the country but what about the white ones?" "It was a scandal!" Professor Hasa lamented. "You could be brought in front of the Party for this!" I asked Professor Hasa if this kind of racism against Roma people was common. "People always insulted the Roma, and they would have felt offended. Roma were given the lower level jobs in society. In Dragot there was just one Roma family, a blacksmith, who was so good that everyone forgot he was Roma. He was a very good man." Thus in Albania, as in other European countries such as Romania, being Roma was often considered as being less than a "good man," and seen as something to be overcome.

As Professor Hasa spoke, the spring swallows swooped low over the road, catching insects to take to their nests. I remembered Majko Majko telling me how he'd had to stand up for himself against anti-Romani insults when he was a young man at *zbor*. We had been enjoying chilled watermelon on a hot summer day, and I had wondered how many stories of the small everyday racist aggressions are forgotten as unpleasant but common occurrences. As in other European countries, anti-Romani racism has worsened in Albania since the end of the socialist period, and the stories of the poorest of the poor remain outside common knowledge.

The sun came out just as we reached the crest of the hill to see the big lake of Belsh glittering below us, surrounded by concrete buildings, with just a few trees on the eastern side. Compared to the spectacular mountains and coasts, this scene was bucolic. Albanian flags flew from the tops of the concrete houses alongside Italian, American and EU flags to symbolize the economic and cultural allegiances of the owners, with a toy animal or plaited garlic nailed to the front of the house to deflect the evil eye.

Professor Hasa told the story of when he taught in Dragot, and had once seen Mehmet Shehu's son in a café in Belsh. Mehmet Shehu was the premier of Albania between 1954 and 1981, when he was found dead in his home. The Party said he was a spy who had committed suicide by shooting himself, while his family believed that the regime had murdered him. The entire Shehu family were arrested and sent into exile. Professor Hasa had known Shehu's son in his Tirana days, but when he saw him in Belsh as an exile with a *Sigurimi* minder he had felt sorry; no one would approach him for conversation, he was an exile amongst exiles. This was the story that came to his mind as we surveyed the city and the lake. Professor Hasa pointed out the school where he had worked for a year, and the vast tracts of land around the lake that had been forests until the 1990s. After the fall of the regime, people cut down the trees for firewood and cleared more land for farming, and now, 25 years later, there is still no adequate garbage collection or road maintenance. "The political parties put new gravel on the roads whenever there is an election campaign," Professor Hasa explained, "but they have never fulfilled their promises to asphalt the road from here on to Dragot."

On the other side of Belsh, and 90 minutes after leaving Elbasan, we stopped for coffee at a petrol station. The faded Marlboro advertising on the flat iron awning marked it as a rusted relic of the early 1990s. Across the road, the abandoned Hunting Club building was surreal proof that there had been forests here, difficult to imagine with barely a tree in sight now. A thin teenager looked bored and depressed as he served us espressos and Coca-Cola in the one-room café with pink walls and pink blinds on the windows. A television in the corner blared a music station from Tirana into the silence.

We drove the last 17 kilometres and parked the car next to a dilapidated building that had been the Party offices. The high road continued on to Vlashuk, but the road downhill to the settlement of Dragot began right in front of us, lined with old and new houses.

View of Dragot, 2010.

Professor Hasa's friends were to meet us in the only café on this main road, which had formerly been the state shop where people queued to buy food, and which was now a bar with an espresso machine. The six square wooden tables in the single-room bar each had four chairs. At one table sat a group of men just a bit older than myself, in their 30s, who stood to greet us. Professor Hasa reached out his hand first, and then we all shook each others' hands. These men were drinking in the morning, and looked as though they had been drinking the night before as well. At another table a tall, old man sat with his wife. He greeted Professor Hasa, but didn't seem to realize who he was.

We sat down at a third table, then Professor Hasa stood up and approached the old man.

"Don't you know who I am?"

"I can't see well anymore."

"Look at me then," he laughed.

The old man slowly raised himself, holding on to the table and brought one eye, cloudy with cataract, close to Professor Hasa's face. Running his eye over every inch of his face he eventually guessed. "Ahhhhh! It's you Riza!" and embraced him.

Professor Hasa's friends arrived in the midst of the loud greetings, and he formally introduced me to them as a historian from Australia writing about "that time."

"Shannon has some questions and the recorder is on!" he said. Unsure of what to say in the public environment, I asked what games they had played as children.

The younger men sat silent and listened to Professor Hasa's well-dressed friends describe how they played together as children, about who was more daring, and who was best at various sports. I asked how old Professor Hasa was when his family came to Dragot (a child), and whether he was accepted by the families already there or socially excluded, and the tone of the discussion shifted. The older men said that everyone got along well, and the other table reacted with uproar.

"Why are you speaking to them about that time? They were the rulers then, and still are now!" one of the young men shouted from the other

table. Everyone was angry and shouting at the same time. The young
men scraped their chairs backwards, their eyes on the older men, while
Professor Hasa's friends shushed them and refused to make eye contact.
"Respect us and let us speak!" they ordered the young men.

"If you speak, you should tell the truth about what happened to
the original Dragot families! Ask them! They know the names of the
persecuted families as well as we do, and we should talk about what
happened to those who were persecuted first!"

"I want to listen to everyone!" I declared. The men fell silent at my
voice in time to hear me repeat, "I want to hear everyone speak."

I don't know whether Professor Hasa said something to his friends or
whether they decided by themselves, but they calmly stood up and left
the bar. I stayed in my place, recorder running, and Professor Hasa said
that he would wait for me outside. I moved my chair over to the table
of the younger men, and through the window I could see the old man
and his wife squatting on the ground across the road. He was chewing a
piece of grass, his cloudy eyes open and alert, peering towards the café.

"No one, no journalist or writer, is interested in our stories," they
told me, "even though we were the ones excluded by the communist
system and by the capitalist system also." These men are angry and hurt
by a lifetime of struggle, and they understand that my questions will
not change a single thing in their hard lives. They are unemployed and
underemployed, working on notoriously dangerous construction sites
and tending small plots of land to feed their families. They were raised
in Dragot as the descendants of politically persecuted internees. The
Party monitored their parents at work and at home, and these were the
children who were not allowed to continue to higher education due to
their inherited biographies. Films and the history curriculum at school
taught every new generation that the "enemies of the people" of the 1940s
and 1950s remained a threat through their descendants. In playground
games these kids were always the bad guys, the *Ballists* or the Nazis,
hunted and defeated by the children who played the roles of communist
partisans, those from families whose biographies were Party approved.

The men calmed as I sat and listened to them. They listed the names of the original Dragot families who had been persecuted by the socialist regime for owning their small plots of land, such as the family with the name Dragoti, linked to the village area through many generations. Their accounts supported those I had read in the history books. When the party had set out to identify the "kulak element" as part of the class war in the countryside in 1949, thousands of families of small land-owners were listed by local communist cadres according to increasingly broad definitions of what a kulak actually was. There weren't many big land owners, and so a kulak was variously defined as someone who owned their own draught animals, employed staff, or who had access to technologically advanced equipment for farming. These people named kulaks were heavily taxed, or their land was confiscated, or they laboured under guard as political prisoners and were then interned in a different village with their family after their release. The atmosphere at the table settled into a resigned hopelessness as we discussed the fact that those who had been powerful as Party members before 1991 had seized the most economic and social capital in the 1990s as well. I asked about their clearly hand done tattoos; they had done them as conscripts in the army in the 1990s.

By the time I thanked the men and took my leave, Professor Hasa's friends had dispersed and were standing around, politely waiting to say goodbye. As I shook hands with everyone and they left, I was struck by how complete the generational transfer of roles was. These men had been sent to Dragot as the children of parents moved there by the Party, albeit as Party functionaries. Today they still represent those who displaced the original Dragot people in the 1950s, although they did not create the system or choose to move there. The interaction between the two groups is clear, each still in the same roles as in the socialist period. It seems to me that the understandable hurt and moral indignation of the formerly persecuted people remains strong because there has not only been no restitution or compensation for the crimes of the past, but also because they are still silenced by the refusal of representatives of the socialist past to listen to their truths, possibly for fear that it would cost them the meagre privileges of social and moral status that they enjoy.

The current school principal walked with us down the hill. The only school in Dragot, for grades one to eight, was on our left facing the apartment blocks. Before 1991 the school had approximately 600 students, but since the state had stopped forcing people to stay in Dragot, the numbers had fallen to 200 pupils. "This is where so much of my life took place," Professor Hasa said as we looked at the carefully maintained but crumbling school building. The overgrown field beside it was a soccer pitch recognizable only by the goal posts, one defended by a grazing horse and the other by a cow. Professor Hasa took my arm and gently pulled me to the side of the road; a tractor coasted down the hill from the main road. "Nooooo braaaaaaakes!" the driver called as he passed, coming to a stop in the field at the end of the street.

Professor Hasa set off at a brisk pace. The road skirted the cluster of apartment buildings and led us to a low set old farm style house at the edge of the village. He knocked on the door as chickens ran around our feet and the turkeys watched us from a distance. "This is the door of the house where I lived when I returned from Tirana, but no one lives here anymore." At the door on the other side of the house an old lady dressed in black with long grey hair plaited and covered with a white cotton shawl answered his knocking. After greeting us with kisses and an embrace, she invited us in but Professor Hasa gently refused, handing her the ground coffee he had brought from Elbasan. I followed him around to the back of the house where the fields began.

"This is the tree. This is the fig tree that my good friend the carpenter planted when he was exiled here in the 1950s. Look how big it is now!" Professor Hasa told me the story of a man whose mill and home were confiscated by the state and who then spent the rest of his life in Dragot under surveillance. The man's children and grandchildren, even those born after he had died, suffered exclusion and discrimination because of their political biographies. Standing under the 60 year-old fig tree, I could see the few kilometres across the fields to the village of Kosovë. This is where the prison for women was built in 1978, and where a dear friend of mine was imprisoned for seven long years. Everyone working in Dragot could have seen her amongst the prisoners walking under guard across the field in silence. These women wore thin shirts and long pants, their old and heavy shovels and picks across their shoulders. When I have asked people in the villages of the region whether they remember seeing the women prisoners, they always do. They remember avoiding long glances, never daring to make contact or conversation with the women; it was not only a possibly punishable offence, but the women reminded everyone of the high cost of persecution.

These women who were imprisoned have names, and each has their own story of persecution. Most were arrested and charged as part of the Party's agenda to intimidate *all* women by shaming and torturing a few; women were simply part of the waves of purge and persecution which was the "class war." In the early 1980s, these prisoners included the 14 Russian women who were married to Albanian men and imprisoned after Albania split with the USSR for fabricated political crimes of spying and agitation and propaganda. The Russian women slept together at one end of the dormitory in the wing of the prison for political prisoners. Others in the political prison wing had been accused of sabotage, spying or of acting as traitors. Some had made mistakes at work, others had not made any mistakes and the accusations against them were entirely fabricated. Some women had ended up political prisoners for having romantic relationships with men accused of maintaining international connections.

In the other wing, for "ordinary criminals," were women who had helped others with home abortions, and women accused of prostitution and theft. There were women who had stolen something small from their workplace such as a swimming costume, and those who had stolen to try to feed their children. There was also at least one woman who could not survive outside in socialist society, and so committed small crimes of theft in order to be returned to prison, where the rules of engagement were clear and she could openly care for her fellow prisoners as she would for her family. When a new prisoner arrived, the women knew that they came directly from a period of torture and interrogation, which often included drugs that induced haemorrhaging and addled the mind. The women who had been nurses at the Psychiatric Hospital in Elbasan before they were arrested and imprisoned for political charges confirmed the suspicions of their fellow prisoners that it was the drugs given during interrogation that induced these effects. They knew this because they had given the same drugs to political prisoners in the Psychiatric Hospital.

Women who were arrested were interrogated by men, and then guarded by men in prison; the threat of rape under interrogation was unrelenting, regardless of whether it was implemented or not. Albanian culture holds the honour of the woman as vital for the honour of her husband's family, and locates that honour in chastity. This means that rape functions as one of the most extreme violations of honour. Thus, fear of rape exists regardless of whether it is perpetrated or not.

As specialists and survivors of torture know, the effectiveness of torture relies on using the social meaning ascribed to certain physical acts, and on using fear and threats in addition to physical abuse. Thus Albanian interrogators used the fear of rape as a torture method in itself. Drita Kosturi, for example, was interrogated and tortured for three years after her arrest in Shkodra in September 1946 on fabricated charges of espionage. She was put to sleep every night as the only woman in a cell crowded with men, in a variety of prisons, and she learnt that all women under interrogation at this time were treated the same way.[8] Drita Kosturi understood, as did many of the men in her cells, that the fear of rape was a tactic intended to keep her in a state of terror. The fear of rape was then, as it remains today in Albanian society, an effective way to terrify all women into submission.

Squinting into the distance I could see in my mind's eye the two rectangular prison blocks that still stand today, operating as a prison for men. I could see the hill behind the buildings where the women buried their jugs of water in the morning to be heated by the sun through the summer days. After ten hours of forced labour, they would wash with the sun-warmed water. While we stood in the gentle spring sunshine, I imagined the tiny outdoor wooden solitary confinement sheds where

8 Susan E. Pritchett Post, *Women in Modern Albania* (North Carolina: McFarlane, 1998), 112.

prisoners were punished. The women would sometimes be beaten there, or, at best, left cramped and alone in the small space. I can't imagine the loneliness these women endured, knowing a colleague or friend had betrayed them and named them enemies of their own people. I thought about the backbreaking labour of agricultural work that everyone did in that time, and about the x-rays that show where the boot of a guard fractured my friend's spine. I thought about the women cleaning the long space of the dormitory, their bunk beds and sagging straw mattresses that curved like hammocks against the walls. For every fig tree that brings the past to the present and links generations of people to a place, there are other pasts, unspoken and without monuments, that haunt us all.

Political prisoner wing of the former women's prison in Kosovë village, Elbasan district, 2010.

"Come, I'll show you something!" Professor Hasa said. We walked back to the main road and through the centre of town again, stopping in front of a tiny square brick building amongst the four-storey apartment blocks. This was the former maternity hospital, the smallest *maternitet* I have seen, with just three rooms. The original roof tiles were broken and sliding out of their places, the doors and windows were bricked in and boarded up. The long ago white-washed external walls are now an archive of graffiti slogans from the 1980s through to today, from "Long Live Enver Hoxha," "PPSH" (the acronym of the Albanian Labor Party, *Partia e Punës e Shqipërisë*) and "Praise the international proletariat" to "hip hop" and "50c," the graffiti artist's mentors for the streets of Dragot after 1991, obviously. The midwife who'd staffed this *maternitet* alone from 1985 onwards had worked 24 hours a day on call when women needed her, and gave injections in the morning and the afternoon. There were three rooms: one for births, one for mothers after birth, and one for the babies. Examinations were conducted in the hall, and fathers of the new-born babies could only see and speak to their wives and new children through the windows. There was no hospital in Dragot, and women were expected to get full treatment for their pregnancies and to give birth at these small and under resourced clinics.

The maternity nurse had been afraid to speak with me, especially as she was being recorded. "I am shaking now to even say these things aloud," she had said, close to tears despite 25 years having passed since the end of the regime. She'd explained that as she came from a family with a bad biography, the Party had closely watched her every move. When her applications to study medicine at university were rejected and she was sent to become a maternity nurse, she'd believed that this was because of her bad biography. The man who was to become her husband, however, had been sent to study medicine and become a doctor even with a bad biography. The statistics published by the Party itself show that they directed women into the lesser paid professions of teaching, nursing and retail, while men were sent to become doctors, engineers and agronomists; the Party at all levels ensured that Albanian women were not able to escape social roles and professions stereotyped as suitable feminine occupations. While Hoxha called on women to emancipate themselves from tradition, the Party actively prevented them from doing so.

Once the midwife began to work, she was sent to Dragot, where her husband worked as a doctor in the same community. She was called to the Party meetings on various occasions to explain why she had stayed an hour or longer in someone's home, and only sometimes did they accept that it was medically vital to run a drip for that amount of time. As with other midwives and nurses in the Dumre region, she knew cases of nurses who had made mistakes and been sent to prison. Every midwife I spoke to told stories of falling asleep with exhaustion in the presence of patients, especially when a labour was long as there was no one to replace them.

Midwives faced a range of unpredictable and potentially lethal problems with every birth, and while there were painkillers and antibiotics available in Dragot, there was no oxygen and no specialist doctor to assist with any problems during a birth. The biggest problem was transporting mothers to hospitals in nearby cities when required. The roads were not sealed, ambulances were few and often lacked the fuel to travel to Dragot and back, especially from Elbasan, and mothers and babies were often in danger by the time a decision was made to request transport. Midwives feared being charged and punished in the case of a mother or baby losing their lives despite their best efforts. One Dumre midwife cried in anguish to remember running kilometres to get to a working radio and phone an ambulance for a woman in labour. The Dragot midwife described the alternatives to ambulance transport.

> Sometimes I could find a tractor, pile hessian sacks on the tray, and transport the mother on top of the sacks. I walked and ran alongside the tractor, wearing boots, and the mud reached to my knees. I always prayed for normal births, so the mother could give birth in the maternity building and so that I didn't need to find transport to get them to a hospital.

"Steel of the Party" Metallurgical Complex opened in 1974, with 13 factories pumping heavy metal smog over Elbasan and the agricultural fields. Pollution flowed downstream through the valley and was fed to the thirsty crops through the irrigation channels. Thousands of men were recruited to staff the Chinese funded industrial complex, and a significant percentage of these workers died from cancerous tumours in the next decades. Midwives throughout the region noted the sharp increase in hydrocephalic and anencephalic babies, and babies born with severe deformities, such as unformed skulls and missing limbs. They used to hide severely disabled babies from their mothers and send the women home without seeing their child. This approach was believed to save the mother extra trauma. Operations to enable the children to live were beyond consideration due to the often severe lack of cranial development, even if there had been surgeons available with the required expertise. Midwives told me that these babies usually died within a few hours or days at the hospital, and that they would not always be counted in infant mortality statistics.

The midwife of Dragot knew women who had died from septicaemia after aborting pregnancies at home (which was illegal), and of young women pregnant with what were called "illegal babies," *fëmijë i paligjshëm*. Once a young unmarried woman came to her with stomach cramps. The midwife's ability to save lives depended on patients trusting her, so the young woman had finally told her what was wrong. Her uncle had made her pregnant, so she had bound her stomach with cloth to hide the pregnancy, then dislodged the placenta at home by herself. She successfully aborted the foetus, but then became very ill with blood poisoning. Knowing that taking this allegation to the Party could result in her own prosecution along with the young woman, the midwife didn't report to any authorities. She told the young woman's parents about the situation, but they chose not to believe her, so the woman was treated for her "infection" and then returned home to the same situation.

On a sheet of metal bolted to the old brick wall of the mechanics centre opposite the *maternitet*, where once the *fletë-rrufes* were pasted for public denunciation, now there was a single word starkly painted in

Maternity clinic, Dragot, 2010.

black. MOS!, meaning DON'T! Holding his hand to shield his eyes from the sun and peering through the admonition, Professor Hasa could make out the original faded slogan words behind it. "I think I painted that one!" The moment was unexpectedly celebratory, as if the distinction between the past and present was firmly established. We took photos standing in front of the multi-layered graffiti walls, and the images show us laughing, our arms thrown around each other's shoulders, temporarily revelling in doing exactly what the wall warned us not to – staring into the past.

As we turned to head back up the hill to the parked car, the school principal joined us again. People returning from their shopping trips of the day stopped to greet Professor Hasa in the street. One thin, old man embraced Professor Hasa and then walked with us for a few metres. He began to softly tell me about how Dragot had not changed for the formerly persecuted people who lived there; the streets still flooded and they didn't have a 24-hour running water supply at home. In front of his

"Don't!" Professor Hasa peers into the past.

Professor Hasa and I at the maternity clinic, Dragot, 2010.

big house, the principal invited us in for a drink, and the old man shook my hand in goodbye. I asked him his name; his family name was Dragoti.

"You have to greet my wife!" the Principal insisted, pulling Professor Hasa with one hand in his and the other across his back. We followed him through the gate and across the bare concrete of the first, open, level of the house. We climbed a concrete staircase bordered with pot plants to the first floor, where we entered the completed rooms of the house through a large metal door. Stepping directly into the lounge room, we slipped off our shoes and stepped onto the polished tiles. The imported Italian lounge suite was set up to face the new television and the view across the school to the mountainous horizon of Berat, rather than down to the apartment buildings of Dragot. The principal's wife served the men raki, and I was grateful for some very nice Italian fruit juice in a small can that I hadn't seen in the shops.

Professor Hasa introduced me at greater length once we sat down. "This is Shannon, she is a journalist writing a book about the communist period. The luminous period of communism!" he intoned with genuine enthusiasm and a touch of mock seriousness. Everyone laughed. "Shannon," he continued, "I have lots of friends. I had friends in that time that I still have today. I would like you to meet a Party secretary from the time of Enver Hoxha. This is the secretary of the Party." I was surprised. "Wow! What work you have done!" I exclaimed.

"We were also forced to work in the fields," the Principal's wife said, while her husband turned to Professor Hasa. "We thought we were smart, but we were just sent to work wherever they wanted us," he laughed.

I was puzzled. Having heard so many stories from formerly persecuted people, I was suspicious of the comparatively luxurious house, but then it was luxurious in the context of the village, far from the urban world. "Was it a stressful position?" I asked the former Party secretary.

"Yes, it was hard work but it was good. We had to meet the production targets. Now people speak badly about that time but there was work, and here in Dragot we realised every plan. We worked a lot, and we realised the plans."

We could have been speaking in 1985, as if the regime had not fallen. Her language was familiar to me from the Party publications praising achievements of the nation, and her voice was confident and projected as if she was reporting to a stranger (which she was) rather than discussing something in her own home with someone she trusted. The men watched while I struggled to think of questions to ask. When I am introduced to someone who held a Party position without them choosing whether they want to speak to me, I worry that I will shame them for their beliefs of the past, especially in a place like Dragot where the "class war" persecuted so many people, almost all of whom were born into the label of "enemy." I am always shocked to meet people who present the socialist period as a positive example of government, and these are always people who had good biographies.

"Did you have *fletë-rrufes*?" I asked.

"Yes, to criticise, but also to praise people who worked well, who did something good."

"What did you think about the *fletë-rrufes* that did accuse people?"

"We just did them. We just did things. For example *aksion*—it was work, but we just did it. Good or bad, we had to do it. But it was good, to my mind."

"And do you remember what happened on the day that Enver Hoxha died?" I asked.

"Because of our education, we had respect for Enver Hoxha, and we cried. I cried alone, and many other people also cried because communism had bad things but also good things. Here in the villages the class war was softer. We worked together, in my opinion. It was good, more safe, in my opinion, especially for women, you could go out alone, safely."

In the silence that followed her answer I held my tongue. I didn't say out loud that it was not safe if you were sexually assaulted by a Party official, or a family member, because no one would help you. I thought of my friend from another Dumre village, whose aunt had fought off the sexual demands of her supervisor at work in the retail industry. He had then accused her of theft, and the Party moved her to hard labour in the agricultural sector with a stained biography. It was not safe for the women who were arrested, interrogated, and imprisoned on fabricated charges of espionage and sabotage, who had to survive years in the prison in Kosovë. It wasn't even safe for women to have children in the region due to the metal factory upwind and upstream of the fields, villages and city of Elbasan.

I held my tongue because I know that people say "it was safer then" because they lived through the 1990s, when Albania was definitely violent and unsafe. In comparison with the 1990s in Albania, the socialist period was safer. As the regime fell, the institutions within which men controlled the behaviour of other men crumbled, such as the police, the army and the Party committees that administered judgements for small crimes. Movement of people ceased to be policed as a criminal offence, men looted weapons from the stockpiles, and some people stole or destroyed what they could. Everyone was deeply confused and emotional; so much was lost with the sudden admissions of the men in power that they had failed to work for the best interests of the people. There was no future for a socialist Albania; the state that had promised protection had betrayed and abandoned the people long ago. The men in power didn't apologise, they got on with the business of consolidating their social and economic capital in the new regime, while the workers they had dictated to fell further into dire poverty, without the cold comfort of ideological illusions.

As in other times, good and honest people had reason to be afraid. Some people known to be informers were attacked, but the vast majority of perpetrators of socialist period violence against innocent people continued to live unafraid and unashamed, taking their coffees in public. Perpetrators of violence in the 1990s primarily targeted the weak. Women walking in the streets were kidnapped and sexually assaulted or trafficked, and men driving cars or shooting guns accidentally killed children as they played outdoors. Pyramid schemes and a refusal of the new leaders to demystify capitalism led to deep anxiety in a confused and traumatised population.

I had heard some stories about the 1990s in Dragot, and I knew that the complexities of the social hierarchy had continued through the painful contests to reconfigure power with physical and verbal force. In this surprise meeting, I decided to keep my questions basic and limited to the socialist period. "What exact work did you do as Party Secretary?" I asked.

"We worked on the plan, a plan for the months and for every day. We ensured that the norms were fulfilled, and we achieved the plans."

"But, concretely, what did you do?" I persisted.

"We did this and lots of other things. We educated women. We held meetings for the women, education for the women, we taught them how to cook, we taught them village life things."

"Like family planning and sex education?" I asked.

She paused. "No. Not that," she guardedly replied.

"How was life for women then?"

"Women had lots of work, of all kinds, state work in the village was organized into squadrons, and in the cooperative it was another form of organization. That's how life was for women. And they had the work at home, more than men. But all families were equal."

She was sticking with the "life was better in that time" discourse. Perhaps if we'd had time alone and she had chosen to speak to me it would have been a different conversation. She had clearly either thought a lot about life being harder for women than for men, or she was just repeating the language of her youth, when Hoxha demanded the "emancipation" of all women.

"Were you afraid in that time?" I asked.

"Of what would I have been afraid?" she coolly responded, looking me directly in the eyes.

"Of anything!" I said, playing dumb. "Wasn't it a scary time?"

"Morally we were afraid, and afraid of making a mistake because in that time they would execute you. But there was also equality. If someone drank a raki, the Committee would call them in to explain why they were drinking a raki. It was a moral fear. And it wasn't just personal, it was for the family—this was even bigger. They punished the whole family."

"Yes," I said. "We met people today who were never treated equally. Generation after generation was persecuted. We can look down from the balcony here and see the homes of these people, they've been there for decades, no?" My comments hit the wall of her eyes and slid to the floor as if unnoticed.

Professor Hasa spoke. "It was a society of 'Do what I tell you to do but don't do what I do,'" but this did nothing to ease the awkward silence. Our hosts kindly invited us to stay for dinner, but we had to get back to Elbasan.

We walked back up the hill to the car in silence. Once on the road, there was a palpable atmosphere of relief and escape, and by Belsh Lake we stopped at a restaurant and ordered a feast of grilled vegetables, cheeses, bread, fried potato, and salad. We were so hungry that we could barely speak until the food came. Over the meal we toasted our hard work with wine.

* * *

The slow drive home was quiet but for the radio. It was twilight as we reached Cërrik and pulled into what looked like a deserted petrol station. A man walked out of the small single-level brick building and Professor Hasa shook his hand. When the man came to the car and leant inside to ask me what I was doing in Albania, I told him I was a historian writing a book about "that time." Leaning into the car from the driver's side, Jeras Naço began to tell me something important.

> We found the bodies just up there, in the ground, and we were sure it was them by their teeth. My father had peculiar teeth – they stuck out. My father and his friend were shot at the same time, and their bodies fell together so we could find them both, together that way.

I climbed out of the car while Jeras continued.

> But what were they accused of? Poisoning the water! But it can't be true because when they were supposed to have met in the anti-state

meeting, he was in the Hotel Turizm in Pogradec! In the trial he said, "Get the registry from there, my name is there, it disproves your information!" But they didn't, and there is no mention of Pogradec in the archival documents, and in the trial you could see he'd been tortured and when the clothes were sent home after the execution you could see on the pants he'd been wearing when they took him, you could see the blood on his clothes and on the waistband you could see the fluid because they had given him injections there, and I don't think they'd fed him. At the trial he was so thin, his head shaved, and so thin. Those trial documents don't mention that when the judge asked him, "If you say now you were in Pogradec, why isn't that written in your statement?" and he answered that by rubbing his wrists.

Jeras's hands caressed his wrists in turn, as if he himself remembered the handcuffs holding him in place.

He rubbed his wrists like this to show he'd been tortured there – that isn't written at all in the archives!

I had met with numerous people whose families had been executed, and this flood of information delivered in a desperate rush was familiar to me. As usual with the stories of the searching children, I hadn't had time to understand the background of the story, let alone ask permission to record it or find my recorder. It was always as if the story existed before and beyond the speaker's conscious choice to share it. Jeras looked at me in expectation. "Do you have archival documents?" I asked. It was all I could think to say – most people hadn't found any kind of documentation at the Interior Ministry offices.

Yes, and 40 photos of the bodies. If you want to see them I can bring them for you. I have 40 photos. There are 40 photos from when we dug and found the bodies.

I told him that I would be honoured to see the photographs, at which Jeras turned to Professor Hasa. "Oh! And I meant to show you!" He hurried inside and returned with a round black plastic tray filled with rocks and shells. He held it in front of him and we gathered around him. He offered the tray of shells and stones to us and we stood there, reached out and touched the small smooth objects. We murmured in surprise at their colours and examined them closely, gently. Jeras spoke to Professor Hasa.

> We found these while digging – they're fossils, pre-historic, shells set in stone or in lava and stones with the shapes of shells imprinted [and] perfectly maintained over time. Are they old? You're the expert in old rocks. Are they old?

Professor Hasa replied that they were about a million years old. Jeras offered us the plate and we reached out, taking the stones one by one, then putting them back. "I don't want to destroy them. I'd like to display them in some way that causes no harm to them."

"No," said Professor Hasa. "That would be beautiful! No, you won't harm them, how could you? They've lasted so long underwater and underground." Picking up single stones we weighed them gently in our hands. Jeras held the tray for us, offering. We chose one, then another. "See how they're perfectly kept after all those years? They're beautiful." ·

Silence took over and we stood for a long time holding the small objects. Finally Jeras put the tray aside. "My father was a good man. He was always correct in his behaviour." With the word correct, he brought his right hand, palm upwards, to the space between us, where the stones had been. He formed a cluster with these upwards-facing fingers then slowly lowered his hand in a straight line through the air. As if his fingers clasped some small truth, he drew us his father's correctness with his hands.

"Do you want to see the photos? When will you come back?" We agreed to meet on Saturday, two days later. As we drove back onto the road we waved goodbye to him, although it was dark and he couldn't have seen us. His words echoed in my mind. "I have 40 photos. Can you see them?"

Chapter Eight

Children of the Lost Generations
- Jeras Naço

Eriada met me at Elbasan Post Office with her sister, Lira, and her ten year old nephew, Irdi. I was tired, nervous, and hungry, and I knew Eriada was also dealing with the intense waves of emotions generated by the interviews we were constantly doing. Lira announced that we would first stop at a swimming pool on the outskirts of Elbasan, and I wondered why we were going to relax when there was so much serious work to be done. As Lira unpacked a picnic breakfast of fresh salad and milk in the shade of the trees, the kids all played together in the water, and I realized that she was looking after us. This is how people care for each other through the memories of the past.

After an hour of calm, Eriada and I went to Jeras's petrol station, not 500 metres from the pool where Lira and the children awaited our return.

* * *

Jeras met us at the door of the small abandoned petrol station. "As soon as I met you I brought everything here so it would be ready to show you."

The room was sparsely furnished, and Eriada and I sat on an old couch, our knees touching the coffee table. In one corner of the room there was a desk with some newspapers on it, and in the other, a small television and a young man watching it. The young man wasn't introduced to us, and he was careful not to disturb our conversation, but he occasionally looked over at us, and I knew he was listening.

I realised later that I could acutely remember the peripheral sound landscape – a canary in a cage outside the door sang its repetitive song, the television soundtrack of a car race was an endless soft roar with jingly commercials at regular intervals. The lack of traffic on the road outside meant that any passing car marked my record of the event both in my memory and on the digital recording.

Jeras is small, compact and energetic. In contrast to the evening we met, when he spoke so fast, he spoke slowly and deliberately in the interview, and his brown eyes were focused on me. He brought over a small brown briefcase, placed it on the table and opened its combination lock. The briefcase was lined with purple velvet, and inside were items wrapped in paper towels. He left the briefcase open, took some pages from a nearby newspaper, laid the newspaper sheets carefully on the coffee table and then removed the items from the briefcase one at a time.

> I will tell you what I have and let you judge if it is worth it or not. This is his passport, his mirror and his spoon from when he was a soldier. You can see them one by one.

He took out a photo album. It played "Happy Birthday" when he opened it, the tinny sound of birthday cards with small batteries. He didn't blink an eye at the incongruence between the happy song and the story he was about to tell. This was the most beautiful photo album to be found in Albania in the mid-1990s, and he handled it gently, as a rare and delicate book.

"I started my photo composition with flowers," he said, showing the first page, a postcard of a bouquet. "But it ends in an ugly way. This is the place where we thought he would be, and there we found him."

The first time we started to work it was almost sixteen days with an excavator as you will see later, but we didn't find anything. We got confused, received some wrong information about the place. During his trial both of them refused the accusations and now the men who killed them cursed them when they told us the name of the place where they were executed. "We killed them like dogs in that place." That is how they said it, word for word.

Do you understand? Wait! Wait!

He jumped up and returned with a book, propping it under the album to lean it gently towards us, reducing the glare of the plastic cover sheets over each photo. I asked how it was that he knew where to dig.

They gave us the information themselves. This is a military zone and people remembered. The olive tree was our orientation point – of course there had been rumours and we knew in our mind exactly where they were buried. This is a picture of the husband of my aunt, and here is where we found them both. The comments we heard over and over from people made us dig everywhere. We did a lot of work for nothing before we found them.
This is the place and this is the excavator digging. These people sitting around are our people, but on some days there would be something like a hundred people coming to watch. Friends, relatives and curious people came for fifteen days until we found them. They came to see what we would find. Then the lies started. People started to say that anyone who knew the exact place would be paid. This person, a friend of my aunt, knew where the place was. The olive tree was the mark for them to remember the place.

Eriada looked upset. I felt the urge to stand up and walk away. I was tired of the incomprehensible cruelty. Every story I hear, with the waves of emotions triggered by forcing a chronology into trauma-shattered time, dissolves my own world also. But can the survivors stand up and walk away? "What about the people that knew," I asked. "How did they know?"

> It was a military zone and around it was the co-operative farm, just two km away from here. Later, the whole thing became a vineyard and people knew that two people had been executed here. So my aunt and others knew, especially this person here, he knew because he worked there for several years. This place is almost 200 metres from the asphalted road to the west. And then lies upon lies, we met with the prosecutor who had handled the case. He got scared but he came with the husband of my aunt, in *besa*, for honour. He gave his word, but still, because he was so afraid, he gave us the wrong information. He said we were digging in the right place. Do you see this? This huge hole. We did it because we thought we would find them here and it is very deep. The deepest dig is this here – we dug the first three metres and then another three metres, and we found the old course of the riverbed. Here we found the water plants, water cane. You know those strong canes? They don't rot in water – you find them here so far down, still here from prehistoric times, under the earth. So when we saw that there was nothing, we continued in other places, as you can see here, also along the road – this is where the prosecutor gave us false information. Here is where we dug six metres. This is my mother, this is my older sister and these two women are the daughters of the friend of my father, who was executed with my father.

As Jeras spoke, Eriada shadowed his deliberate words with a gentle, lilting English translation. She spoke too softly for me to clearly hear, but Eriada is an emotionally present and instinctive translator. Her voice soothed Jeras, and reminded me that we had time and the ability to hear him. Jeras looked at me. "It must have been hard," I murmured. Unintentionally, perhaps from my own feeling that there were no words to respond, my tone was questioning. Jeras stopped his page turning, stared at me, and with a shift of emotion to a controlled anger said, "Why would you ask me that?"

Five seconds of silence passed and, as if shocked by his outburst, without losing eye contact, he quietly said, "There is no need to ask." I reminded myself that I would not walk away while Jeras shared his experience, and when I glanced at Eriada I saw that she had also somehow steeled herself. She nodded at me and blinked reassurance. Jeras returned his eyes to the photos, wounded.

> Again with the digging. As you can see here, again and again in every dig we would stay to watch. Look here how deep we dug. This is the husband of my aunt, and this is the representative of the Organization for the Integration of the Formerly Politically Persecuted. He dealt with different things and arrangements at that time. Look how deep this is. This is my daughter. These pictures were taken in 1993–94. We were emigrants in Greece when my aunt summoned us, and we raced back home to search for the bodies. This is when we stopped working, around six in the afternoon after finding the bones. And the last picture in this album is the sunset. This is how I chose to end this album.

He pauses, looks lost, and I ask, "Are there many people searching for lost bodies?"

"Yes, there are a lot of people. This person here is still searching for his father," he says, pointing into a crowd photographed waiting beside an excavated hole. There are many, but for me, maybe, I think, I think I am not wrong, but suppose I am mistaken? Are these the bodies of my father and his friend? For me, at least, the regime was very precise and the documents can be found. Maybe now in democracy the documents don't have the value they had during the regime time, now you can buy a document or a stamp. Do you understand? Back then, those who signed the documents signed the documents, yet now these same people say that it wasn't true."

He picks up an envelope full of photos, still in the packet from the photo shop. Standing up, he ruffles through them. He chooses one, then flips to another. Finally he sits and starts to quickly put them one after another in a pile on the table. I reach out to touch them, to show that I can bear to linger on the images if he can. These are the photos of the bones being excavated and cleaned.

> These are the bodies of my father and his friend as we found them in the ground. See how awkwardly they lie? How they lie across each other? This body position shows how they were killed. Here you can see it from different angles.
>
> This is where we took them out to re-bury them together. This is the clearest picture of them both, how we found them. This is where we started to put them together.
>
> And this is after we cleaned and composed them. The position they were buried in shows that they were killed on the ground, kneeling. My father was shot first, not in the skull, but in the back of the neck, like this, here.

He points to the back of his own neck.

"And it came out here," he says, moving his finger to the front of his neck.

> And he fell into the hole and then his friend was shot, and then just pushed down the hole. He fell on top of my father and they were buried like this – their legs are entwined and the bones are shattered.

"Who are these men who are cleaning with you?" I ask.

> This is me, this is my uncle, this is another friend, this is my cousin, this woman is the wife of my father's friend. These are all family members, when we found the first signs of the bodies. We returned two days later and started to clean them – we used spoons and knifes, that was all we had, and with a lot of care we removed their bodies together. Time did not move them. We could

see how strangely the two bodies lay, one hand over the hips, one on the shoulders of the other as if one was climbing. They lived 30 years underground together.

We found a pair of shoes, but did not know who they belonged to. Their shoes were not on their feet, but we also found synthetic socks and a shirt of the same material that belonged to the other man. He had escaped to Yugoslavia, from there to Bulgaria or Romania, and from there he came back. Actually, he tried to reach the Soviet Union – he was obsessed with it. Together with his family – with his wife, two daughters and two sons – all of them escaped. He was not given a visa in those countries, so he came back. Even though he was warned that he would be imprisoned, he didn't care. He said he knew he was going to be punished, but at least he would bring his family back to their own country. They came here. Of course, they knew he was coming from the moment he sailed from the Black Sea, and even before reaching the Albanian shore he was captured by the *Sigurimi* boats. He was sentenced to 12 years for treason and escaping, you know, the same recipe they used on everyone else. Not even six months after being sentenced and imprisoned, he was sent back to the prosecutors and, together with my father, they gave him another sentence and executed them both.

Of course, we recognized the synthetic clothes because they were bought outside the country; here in Albania they did not exist. There were no such clothes in Albania. So we took those clothes and put them in little boxes. This is his son. We could recognize my father by his teeth, his front teeth. He had very distinctive front teeth – everyone remembers them – and we knew then that this was him. We took them to the municipality because other bones were found. When almost twenty people had been found, a big ceremony was given in their honour before they were re-buried. My father and his friend and then twenty others were buried together in the same plot in the cemetery. That is all they did, a ceremony. That is not enough for him.

"Did your family start searching as soon as the regime was over?" I ask.

> Listen, even though people told stories about his execution, we still felt he was alive because we expected that anything could come from communism. The politics were such that everything was enigmatic. So even though people would say he was killed, we thought maybe he was left alive. We knew that they had improvised the trial, made it like a play! We all knew him, my father. He was not a bad man, so, maybe, we thought, it was all fabricated. There was always a question mark [as to] whether he was killed or not. Until we found the bones, we still hoped he was alive. So this is how we ended up where we are today, where we are now, through a lot of effort and pain. Personally, I have questioned the meaning of my own existence. If I had known before that he was dead, at least I would not have experienced this torture.

There is such a long pause between when Jeras finishes talking and the questions I ask. Eriada's body is sinking into itself, growing smaller, and her sadness, or maybe mine, makes me think that she is blurring at the edges. I want to leave and I don't want to know more, but I grip my legs with my hands – I need to be able to fully hear what Jeras is struggling to explain.

"Jeras, why didn't you take revenge?" I ask.

The young man watching television looks over at us and doesn't look away, shock on his face. Jeras softly says, "Thank you," his right hand on his chest, and he pauses.

"I want to tell you something. If, for example, you insult me now, I am personally able to distinguish between us and say that only your conscience knows what your intentions are 100%. But for me, because of my culture and my soul, the question is whether you acted against me with autonomy or because you were forced to act in that way. I have this question with me all the time and I think that 99% of torture was imposed by the regime and just this 1% was on an individual's conscience. And I leave it to God to deal with you. I cannot become a criminal. Yet this is hard. Today, even now, the person who divided people by labelling them the enemy class is the head of an association for the formerly politically persecuted people to claim their rights. What he broke to pieces in that time, today he gathers and binds, and he makes this his job.

Do you understand?"

"Yes," I say.

"Do you really understand?"

"I understand," I say.

"I know you are listening, but I want to know if you really understand me. I would be really glad if you could understand me 100%."

I look to Eriada. She gently shrugs, almost imperceptibly. Her eyes look tired. Jeras has not moved his eyes from mine. What can I say? He is asking if I understand because he knows that no one can really understand – he can't "understand" all of this either. I turn my body towards Jeras and touch my right hand to my chest, my eyes on his, and this says enough. We sit and share the space with our eyes. I don't feel like a historian – I can't imagine facts strong enough to illuminate how humans can do this to each other.

Words come in their own time.

"What would justice look like for you now?" I ask.

My father and all the others like him were punished by the law and the state. In the same way the state punished them, in the same way, the state should put their dignity where it belongs, the state and no one else. If I was asking to do justice myself, the state should not allow me, saying that it is a state obligation to make justice. What do you think?

I reply that I don't know; I'm not him, I'm not a politically persecuted person. He interrupts me.

No, I meant something else with my question. You have heard many stories, so in your conscience you should feel, in this position you are in now, maybe I am wrong, but you also should feel like

a victim. My question is what do you think about my answer in
your point of view? Can you tell me where justice is?

I am struck by the question. What does it mean that he asks this? Is it a
rhetorical exercise to show me that the question cannot be answered? In
the role of historian I am not meant to be asked how I "feel" about what
I learn, although this uncomfortable space of feeling the past of others
is where I spend most of my time. I fear that I cannot hold the space for
us to speak about what happened in his life if I also begin to speak of
my own relationship with the injustice, so I offer an academic response.
"I don't have hope for a state response, in my opinion, even when Berisha
sets up a commission for investigating crimes under communism, I think
it will be dirty from the beginning. I would love for this to be possible,
but I don't think it will happen.'

I stand on my solid ground and he remains with me, we share the
labour of weaving words around the edge of the abyss. Together we are
finding words to draw attention to what cannot be put into words.

Maybe we should not mention the names of the politicians as they
come and go, but the real politics, the one at the core that cannot let
the truth come alive. Do you understand me? Albania is a fucked
up place. Please understand what I mean. The regime was so mean
and so cruel – it's beyond expression. I could never be educated and
I regret that, but this is life. I loved learning but at the age of ten
I was forced to stop. I had to undergo my destiny. My conversation
now is just one piece of a million of the whole. What I want to
express is the joy of speaking with you, Shannon – Shena – let's say
it in Albanian. Look, this is just a small part of the whole; I never
had the ego to make my own story the most important of them
all. I am giving you information, specific information, but in a
general way. I have told you the reality, but how you put it in your
own words depends on your own perspective of the big picture.
You are not working just for me or for another person like me.
I understand you very well, I have understood you since the first

day we spoke. My joy is to be part of the whole story in your book. Of course, I understand sincerely. It's my human nature, and your standpoint is the same. Above all, I am saying to you I cannot impose anything on you. My own pleasure in talking to you is one thing, but you will act for your own pleasure and according to your own will. I am happy to express what I experienced to you – even just talking to you brings me joy. And if you will make it a part of the whole, then this is another different joy, a beautiful memory. This is a two-way relationship. I think I am not mistaken.

"You are not mistaken," I answer. My centre of balance starts to slide. Jeras has exposed the heart of the work I do. History and justice are only words, and here they mean haunting. The question of what would constitute justice now is the question of how to live with the haunting. Jeras recognises that he cannot control what I write, and so he invokes the vulnerability we share as humans in the face of death, the questions of what a life can "mean," what a loss can "mean." I am terrified at the prospect of how we can communicate, between and outside of ourselves, without what is promised by "writing history," but Jeras can say it straight. We remain each ourselves, parts of the whole. Every history is likewise a fragment, a part of the whole which we can never see in its entirety, let alone control or predict.

* * *

"Can I ask some specific questions? Which documents did you find?" Jeras's body relaxes. He leaps up and shouts, "YES! You should ask me!" He takes the documents from the briefcase and waves the stapled bundle of photocopied pages in the air. "You have to ask me! Because maybe I will say something else, something different!"

This is our shared hope, that there will be clarity, that ghosts can be soothed. Through coming to know some things together, we trace what cannot be known in this space, the anguish that fills the whole space at other times. We speak.

Jeras's father, Apostol Naço, was born in 1930 in a village called Nifol, outside Vlora. His parents were named Ndino and Sofia. He had five years of school and the communists categorized his class origin as "poor shepherd," but he finished all his school classes and worked in the technical profession of veterinarian. He married and had five children. Apostol Naço was arrested on 19 February 1966, tried in court on 18 August 1966 and executed between one and two months later. No one knows exactly when the execution took place, because the state did not inform the family then, and has not given any information to the family since the fall of the regime.

> This is the sentence given to my father. I can read you just the end of it. These are not his words. I am 100% sure of it! I am calm and realistic when I say this. The scene that happened in the trial… when my father said, "I could not have organized the collection of poison for the water supply because I was at the tourism hotel in Pogradec – bring the registry of the hotel and you will have my evidence," does not exist anywhere in this transcript.

The Party wrote the trial before it was held.

> Yes. It was a public trial. They did it in the *Pioneri* Cinema in Elbasan. You know the cinema?

I nod. I am listening. Jeras's voice drops to just above a whisper and he speaks very slowly.

> [The trial] was announced with loudspeakers in the city. It was well organized. The room was full of people and the crowd outside could listen to what was happening on the loudspeakers. I wasn't allowed to go in. I was only 10 and my family didn't let me go in. They brought the prisoners to the trial in trucks so big that the guards brought chairs for the prisoners to climb down like stairs. Their arms and legs were tied with chains. My father

and Niko were always together, and both of them rejected the accusations of the court. They said that Niko had been the chief of the anti-Party group, and when he had escaped, as I mentioned before, he had left my father in his place. This is how they came to face court together.

"But what group did they say he was the chief of?" I ask.
"Oh! You don't know the accusation! Look here!"

He laughs, excited again. He reads fast, tripping over his words as he gets to the name of his father. The language of the document is circuitous, socialist period legalese.

"The Jury of Durres–Elbasan is composed by Secretary Hajrie Zhuka, with the participation of the prosecutor Hys Zaja and in presence of the Defence attorney Ndoc Sheldija for the defended Niko Hito and attorney Avni Skrapari for the defended Apostol Naço, on the trial session of 18.07.1966 to issue the accusations against the defendants."
The sentence: "I declare you Niko Hito guilty of treason against the country, with your participation in the anti-Party group as expressed in the Penal Code 64.29 for economic sabotage, illegal group activities and according to law 22.96 I sentence you to 20 years prison. In joint crimes as the law states you are condemned to death by gunfire and removal of the decorations given."
For Apostol Naço: he is charged with treason against the country, participation in an illegal group and is sentenced to death and then it says: "crime and economic sabotage in association" and he is sentenced to death by gunfire.
So! The charge was "collaboration with an enemy group against the people's government," collaboration with foreign espionage agencies, Greek and Yugoslav. Economic sabotage means that it involved the misuse of socialist property. So he was sentenced to 25 years for collaboration, then18 years for espionage, 20 years

for sabotage, and all of them together he was sentenced to death. So the accusation was political and economic enemy activities against the state and espionage.

His voice drops to a whisper and slows again.

Six months passed between the arrest and the trial. We knew he was in Elbasan.
Once a fortnight my family sent him clothes and food. He and my mother never met. The only child who was sent to take it was the son of my aunt, who is not living anymore, and he was six years old. That child was the only one who was allowed to enter the cell and meet with them. During the six months before the trial no one could see him. The day of the trial, my mother and he saw each other in court. My relatives took the front row of seats and watched them sitting just behind the bar. As for me, I was outside – I was a kid. I could see him only when he arrived and left the trial.
And... The last moment I remember seeing him, and I can't forget, was after he received the sentence. They were put in the truck—

Jeras speaks slowly and he's crying, as if someone is squeezing his stomach from inside. Our eyes remain fixed on each other.

and they stepped in it and sat like this...

Jeras sits on the floor, crouches, his knees against his chest, his hands as if bound by the wrists around his knees.

My father was on the left. His friend was on the right, and my father was sitting like this.

Jeras lowers his head to his knees. He sits as his father was forced to sit.

My aunt took me.

He gets up from the floor and sits beside me again. "It was the same distance between me and that plant," he says, pointing to the corner of the room, "and I had my head shaved, like you, and she took me and put her hands on my head, like this."
He puts his hands firmly on my head, his face is close to mine.

My Aunt told me, "Look at your father!"
You see?
He was sitting there...

He slowly takes his hands from my head. In a long silence between us an advertisement on the TV plays some happy love song jingle.

After two months they were executed.

"Are you sure he was held in the psychiatric hospital in Elbasan?" I ask.

Yes.

I have searched in their archives. I managed to enter downstairs and the nurses told me. At that time we knew that his underwear was full of blood in the place where doctors usually give injections, below his hip. It is absolutely certain, and he also said it during the trial, that he accepted false things written in the statement because he was being beaten. It was under pressure that he agreed he had met a person considered an enemy of the state, then during the trial they were not handcuffed, he was just sitting there on a chair, and he told them he had never met that person. The judge said, "But in the prosecutor's office you said something else," and my father rubbed his wrists and nodded towards the prosecutor, "Ask that person why I said it this way."

Jeras rubs his wrists again as he tells the story.

> My father spoke little – it was his character. He spoke few words but he measured what he said. He was badly tortured. He was not given food. And then, after two months, when they were executed, my aunt went there with food and she was given back a bag of my father's clothes, along with his shoes and personal effects. My mother still has them today, as they were then.
>
> Immediately after the trial the government sent us to Kosovë. We were taken there and we were under surveillance. The psychological violence was non-stop, twenty-four-seven. The psychological war never ceased, and my friends were always warned not to associate with me, not to come to my house or even be seen with me. I was so ashamed because of this. Intentionally or not those people even doubted my politeness – they said I acted politely because I was an enemy of the state, not because it was my character. The politics of communism were to divide and conquer – they used wives against husbands, brothers against brothers or sisters, sons against fathers, so the person felt like a cane in the wind.

"Why did they persecute your father?" I ask.

> My father was an intellectual and civil servant, and he was well known. Communism was structured in that way – they physically punished those who were well known as a psychological punishment for the masses. It was a perfectly structured system that kept power for 50 years. Because my father was punished with execution, everyone who knew him expressed their feelings for him to me over the years and, in this way, accumulating their words, I have built this character of my father. I put all the parts together and from other people's words I have created in me his way of thinking. This is why I am speaking so passionately. He grew up with me. People say that he was a good man, a correct man, and this was why he was punished.

They even lied in order to arrest him. The vice director came in the evening and told him, "Apostol, tomorrow we have a meeting at the Ministry of Agriculture," and they arrested him in Rrogozhina. They told him to show up in the morning, then there were three *Sigurimi* waiting for him. They said, "In the name of the people, you are arrested!" Two days later they came to the house and searched everything. They took his diaries, documents and postcards. My brother and I had a collection of 80–100 postcards people had sent us. They said they would bring them back but they never did. What was left of him was hidden, and I brought these things here to show you.

I thanked Jeras for showing me everything, and he thanked me for coming.

"I have to go back to a point in our conversation," he said. "You asked me how justice would look for me today. The heavy feeling that I can't answer that, or even grasp what it would look like, was relieved by talking to you. I feel relieved because the dignity of my father is being put in place by being part of your book."

We watched Jeras wrap his father's passport, his mirror, and his spoon in tissue paper. He put them back in the briefcase one by one, closed the briefcase, and sat down again.

Apostol Naço as a young man.

Conclusion

Eriada and I drove back to Lira and Irdi at the swimming pool. The effect of listening to Jeras share his story was familiar to me; it felt as if all the structures of existence, time, and meaning in the present, had dissolved. In English we sometimes refer to grief as a well; a narrow, dark, deep place where we are alone, inescapably disorientated. Far from others, far from the surface of life, somewhere in the depths, the well of grief is of another world, separate. You can't step out of it because you don't even know how far you are from the surface. This place of grief is a reality. Jeras had met Eriada and I on the surface of his own grief, and he had trusted us to wait for him, listening, while he descended into the dark space alone and shared his life story with us. Through listening closely to Jeras's experience, I had shared his experience of the loss and grief myself and found myself in the other-worldly space where the losses of the past constitute the dominant present.

Lira saw us and began the work of bringing us back, as families do all over Albania. While she laid out the salad and handed us bread, she questioned Eriada with her eyes, and Eriada responded with a slow shake of her head. Lira commanded us to eat. Calling Irdi for lunch, the children's voices spoke of games and dares and success. I became aware of the sun burning my skin although I didn't feel it as such. I perceived depth and emotions in the noises around us, but I felt as if I was in the Pioneer's Cinema with Jeras, horrified, watching Apostol Naço step down from the truck. With every return I bring new ghosts, new geographies of places and times that haunt my own everyday life, and may now haunt yours also.

When I hear someone say "we were all equal then" about the communist period in Albania, the ghosts make themselves present in the racing of my heart. I try to calmly point out that the socialist government retained control by continually persecuting some people as undeserving of equality. Some of those whom the Party deemed "the people" named others "enemies of the people;" the women and men imprisoned on fabricated charges of political crimes, those named kulaks, *Ballists*, and their grandchildren, born four decades later. The system relied on perpetual "class war," and retaining one's right to "equality" relied on the exclusion of others from the same treatment. Some were equal only because everyone lived in fear of being made desperately unequal.

The people we have met in this book are outstanding in their desire to wholeheartedly engage with their pasts as individuals shaped by living in communist Albania. Taking Jeras's briefcase as metaphor, we can reflect on how each individual brought their own briefcase carrying their past to our conversations. They unpacked their memories, held them in the light of our conversations, and put them away again to resume their life in the present. Through their patience, courage, and trust, I have learnt about what life was like in that time, and how people carry their memories of events through time and present them to us.

In the first section of the book we met Thoma and Mevlude, who lived through the duration of the communist regime in Albania, with deep understandings of what came before and after. Their snapshot of the world before communism included Thoma's family of shepherds building their business, connected to Vlach, Greek and Italian communities and trade, and Mevlude's father's determination to build a stronger Albania through education and democracy. Mevlude and Thoma watched their parents to learn how to work within the ideology of the incoming socialist government in the 1940s. Mevlude's father took the language of free elections at face value and was arrested for his efforts, resulting in Mevlude's life labelled with a bad biography. Thoma's family negotiated the waves of legislation and restrictions by submitting in public and resisting in private. As a young man, Thoma was idealistic and vocally supportive of the Party until his superior directly told him that the language of the ideology was not the reality and never would be, but to never admit this.

Thoma and Mevlude are both sincere and hard working people, and it was precisely those traits that threatened the people maintaining the system. One mechanism of Party control was enforced acquiescence to mediocrity in management. In Party meetings, Thoma pointed out the cruelty of him judging the supposed crimes of others when he was not trained in law, and Mevlude's vital role in chemical production despite her biography illuminated the system's preference for Party faithful over professionally competent people. The socialist system was not a meritocracy, and anyone who spoke a critical truth was persecuted. Thoma was punished with prison and surveillance, Mevlude with exclusion from professional and social trust.

The Party gained power through the arbitrary punishment of individuals, which seeded distrust and fear within families. Individuals had to be constantly on guard because a person or the Party could accuse them of any fabricated or exaggerated charge without warning. The *Sigurimi* arrested people without notice, or they disappeared without a trace, leaving a bewildered and grieving family with a bad biography and a life of persecution. As we see in Thoma and Mevlude's life experiences, this tactic of divide and rule was used against the families of ordinary people and affected the vast majority of families in a population of just 3.2 million people.

Diana and Liljana were born into the established regime and so were born into their parents' careful silence. They had to navigate the difference between rhetoric and reality for themselves as they grew up. When Diana deliberately dirtied her special dress for the Muslim celebration of Eid to emulate the Chinese heroines of the Cultural Revolution, her mother sighed in sadness. Diana noticed, but believed that she was following the correct path of the Party. The regime benefitted from the convictions of youth, and exacerbated the tendency of each new generation to blame the one before for their mistakes. When Diana's father himself was a victim of the regime's relentless purges, Diana was conflicted. She believed that her father had the interests of the people at heart in any criticisms he may have made, but she also wanted to believe that the Party was just. When her friends suddenly excluded her, Diana realised that socialist equality was a beautiful myth available only to those with good biographies, and she no longer felt safe in the country that she had been prepared to fight for.

As undeniably working class people, Lili's family appreciated being close to power in that her grandfather's work as a gardener for Politburo members afforded him special treatment. Lili was able to attend school with the children of powerful socialists because of her grandfather's connections, and she had no illusions about the fact that socialist society remained hierarchical. When Selim had wept at the purging of Minister Deliana, he was shushed and bustled into another room. Lili understood that to maintain a life free of political persecution, one had to be silent and display blind faith in Party decisions.

Without any special connections, Lili and Majko were refused permission to live with their own children; their good biographies and work for the Party were not enough for them to be awarded treatment equal to others in the same position. When they were finally moved closer to Majko's family, after a longer time than other teachers had to suffer far from their families, they were still not allotted an apartment but shared the overcrowded home of the Majko family. It is not possible to say without a doubt that socialist state policy was to refuse higher education to the siblings of Majko and Lili because they wanted to keep Romani and Egyptian Albanians socio-economically marginalised, but this was certainly the effect, and it happened to many Romani and Egyptian families.

The Party claimed to emancipate all workers from ethnic stereotypes and marginalisation, just as it claimed to emancipate women from patriarchal control. In reality, however, the Party perpetuated pre-existing hierarchies of ethnicity and gender in order to maintain social control and engineer population increase and economic growth. There were only two female Politburo members between 1948 and 1990; it was men who criminalised contraception and abortion to make all women work to produce more Albanian workers. Just as it was the Party, predominantly men, who forced women into lesser paid, feminized professions and reproduction and called it "emancipation." It was the Party members and people at all levels of society that actively segregated Romani and Egyptian Albanians into lesser paid professions.

The final section of the book focused on how the recent past remains with us in the relationships and physical landscapes of the present, through the life stories of Professor Hasa and Jeras Naço. These men now devote themselves to the painful task of recovering history with tenderness and courage. For Jeras Naço, the order of nature was reversed when he lost his father as a child, and when he shares this experience we feel first hand the reversal of time; the traumatic past interrupts the present. Indeed, the trauma continues now, as the major political parties hide information about the past and stymie procedures for restitution and compensation.

As we saw when we visited Dragot, the descendants of both the formerly persecuted workers and the former perpetrators of persecution are locked into inherited positions of blame, injury, and defensiveness. This is painful for all parties, although it is the formerly persecuted who are most violently disregarded by the Albanian media, government, and society now. State and social disregard for those who were formerly politically persecuted is primarily motivated by fear. If state representatives address historical injustices, then the post-socialist actions of men from both political parties who have acted for their own wealth at the expense of the everyday Albanian people they claim to represent will also have to be acknowledged as unjust. The majority of people, those who work hard and worry about their children, have been exploited and treated badly by post-socialist governments just as they were by the socialist regime.

And yet, under inescapable, unpredictable, and ruthless state control, even those most persecuted by the regime resisted. People focused on developing their professional skills and working as well as they could, on educating their children, and treating others with respect regardless of the risk it posed to oneself. Families cared and still care for each other through nightmarish sagas of loss and suffering. Individuals refused to inform on or denounce both loved ones and strangers, and people tenderly hid signs of their "illegal" beliefs at the back of the closet or in jokes they never said out loud. Some individuals thought deeply about their situation in the privacy of their own minds, and others avoided thinking deeply in order to bring their sincerity and hard work to the tasks the Party forced them to do. Most people did all of these things.

Many still wait for explanations and apologies, and some are waiting to apologise, but they speak. People continue to share memories of their daily fears, trials and ambivalent feelings despite the focus of media and mainstream discourse on political events and the lives of the elite. As Mevlude pointed out, the power of those excluded from position or privilege is not a moral claim earnt through suffering, it is the power of knowing that the meaning of life is not wealth or notoriety. Meaning is made through sincerely knowing oneself in the human context of family and friends, and there is meaning in how we are haunted today by those we could not save from the injustices of the Albanian regime. In this way, every conversation about the socialist past in the violently unjust capitalist present, every history documenting what was created and what was destroyed in the time between 1944 and 1991, is an act of remembering which makes meaning and community now.

Acknowledgments

Thank you to the hundreds of people who looked me in the eyes and told me what had happened. On streets, in buses, while shopping, when you overheard me speaking with someone else at coffee and leant over to touch my arm and begin, thank you for your trust and sincerity. Sincere thanks to Thoma Çaraoshi, Mevlude Dema, Diana Keçi, Liljana and Majko Majko, Professor Riza Hasa and Jeras Naço. When you shared your stories with me, each of you shared intelligent and deeply considered interpretations of events, giving insight into your singular life histories and illuminating the bigger picture of Albanian society in general. I must also say that I take all responsibility for any perceived inconsistencies in my presentation of these histories.

I thank Eriada Çela, Besa Lushaj and Edlira Majko, for their wonderful work as research assistants. Thank you also to Sonila Danaj and Sonila Muzhaq. Your excellent skills of translation, transcription and research over the years have been priceless. I thank Gjergj Erebara, Artan Hoxha and Luljeta Ikonomi for their enthusiastic interest in the questions I have had about Albanian history, and Luljeta for such wonderful academic collaboration. You are all blazing intellectuals with integrity and compassion and I am humbled and inspired by the work you each do.

In the early years (2003-2006), Frank Dalton, Sonila Danaj, Xhulieta Harasani, Luljeta Ikonomi, Blendi Kajsiu and Danjela Shkalla and their families opened their homes to me and did the hard work of teaching me how to speak and also how to listen. I thank you all for your support in work and in friendship. While your stories are not written here, I could not have heard any others without yours, and they remain close to, constitutive of, my heart. You are all a vital part of my story.

Many close friends in Albania enabled me to undertake and complete this work over the years. I thank the Ikonomi - Çaraoshi family and the Çela family, especially Eriada, Lira and Irdi. Thank you to Artemisa Çelani and her family, Xhulieta and Petrit Harasani, Anduena Shyti, Ruth Kelly, Ela Deneku and Frank Dalton. Thank you all for the conversations, laughter and love that we have shared over the years. Thank you to Idrit Idrizi, Albana Rexhepaj and Irida Vorpsi for their academic work and for the recent volume of *Perpjekja* bringing together so many amazing scholars. To my everyday Albanian-history-world-through-the-internet people, thank you to Xhuli Agolli, Aurora Guxholli, Xhodi Hysa and Ylli Tabaku, for always answering questions with thought provoking conversations. Each of you has things to say that no one else can write. Please write books.

Outside Albania, I have benefitted from the support of my family, especially Carol and Tony Woodcock, and the friendship of many amazing people, all of whom do work that makes the world a better place. I thank Åsa Jansson, Crystal McKinnon, Joseph Toltz, Anna Keber, Marcela Brassett, Roland and Laura Clark, Sacha Davis, Ken Lee, Sarah DeSantis, Carolyn D'Cruz, Adam Driver, Monika Flaschka, Jodi Frawley, Litea Fuata, Damir Mitric, Seide Ramadani, Jordy Silverstein and Shahla Talebi for valuable collaborations, friendship, and conversations over the years. Special thanks to the visionary and indefatigable Alex Lambevski and Mark Walbank at Sextures Institute, no better colleagues exist. I am grateful to Åsa, Sacha, Dorothy Maniero, Blendi Kajsiu, Jacinta Butterworth and Heidi Beattie for helpful comments on various drafts of the manuscript, and to Dorothy Maniero for map-making at the right times. Faleminderit to Silvana Çuni, who has been a constant friend, inspiration, and teacher of all things. Silvana, Anamaria Beligan, Chris Fontana and Venetia Gillot are an outstanding group of fun and smart women who write—I wouldn't like Melbourne much at all without their laughter and voices in it. I would also like to thank Karl Armstrong and Philip Court for their sincere and nuanced reflections on Albanian history and the history of hopeful action.

Finally thanks to the wonderful people at HammerOn Press who literally made this book. Thank you to Eva Megias for the book cover design putting Albanian women in their rightful-visible-place, and I thank Natalie Brown for proofreading. Thank you to Deborah Withers for finding the play and being able to hear, and for being the kind of editor one reads about in acknowledgements sections; organised, effective, and revolutionary.

The cover photo is Liljana Majko (left) and a friend standing outside Elbasan University in 1973. As neither cameras or cars were privately owned under the socialist regime, Lili and her friend are posed here with the car of the University Director. State photographers often took portraits in popular locations so that people could have their photo taken, and then collect the print later from the studio.

References and Further Reading

This book was based on oral histories recorded and archived in the possession of the author. Below are selected references, predominantly in English, for further reading about Albanian History, socialism, and everyday life studies, and oral history methodology and trauma.

Albanian History

Abrahams, Fred C. *Modern Albania: From Dictatorship to Democracy in Europe*. New York: NYU Press, 2015.

Amnesty International *Albania: Political Imprisonment and the Law*. London: Amnesty International, 1984.

Anonymous. *Anthology of Wounds: A Terrific and Artistic Testimony of the Hell of the Living*. Tirana: Albanian Rehabilitation Centre for Trauma and Torture survivors, 2004.

Arbnori, Pjeter. *The New Martyrs in Albania: 10300 Days and Nights in Communist Prisons*. Translated into English by Elvana Thaçi. Tirana: Enti Botues Poligrafik "Gjergj Fishta," 2004.

Bekteshi, Vera. *Vila me dy Porta (The House with Two Doors)*. Tirana: K & B, 2009.

Biberaj, Elez. *Albania in Transition: The Rocky Road to Democracy*. Boulder, Colorado: Westview Press, 1998.

Blumi, Isa. "Hoxha's Class War: The Cultural Revolution and State Reformation 1961- 1971." *East European Quarterly* 33 (1999): 303-326.

Blumi, Isa and Hakan Yavuz, M. *War and Nationalism: The Balkan Wars, 1912-1913 and their Sociopolitical Implications*. Salt Lake City: University of Utah Press, 2013.

Blumi, Isa. "An Honorable Break from Besa : Reorienting Violence in the Late Ottoman Mediterranean." *European Journal of Turkish Studies* 18 (2014). https://ejts.revues.org/4857 Accessed January 5, 2016.

Clayer, Nathalie. "Behind the Veil: The Reform of Islam in Inter-War Albania or the Research for a 'Modern' and 'European' Islam." In *Islam in Inter-war Europe*. Edited by Nathalie Clayer and Eric Germain. 128-155. New York: Hurst, 2008.

De Waal, Clarissa. *Albania Today: A Portrait of Post-communist Turbulence*. London, New York: I.B.Tauris, 2005.

Dyrmishi, Demir. *Lufta Politike në Udhëheqjen e PKSH (PPSH) 1944-1960*. Tirana: Toena, 2011.

Elbasani, Arolda and Artur Lipinski. "Transitional Justice in Albania: Historical Burden, Weak Civil Society, and Conflicting Interests." In *Transitional Justice and Civil Society in the Balkans*. Edited by Olivera Simic and Zala Volcic, 105-121. New York: Springer, 2013.

Elsie, Robert. *Historical Dictionary of Albania*. Lanham: Scarecrow Press, 2010.

Erebara, Gjergj. "Elementi Demografik në Krizën Ekonomike të Viteve '80." *Perpjekja* 32–33 (2014): 110-128.

Fischer, Bernd. *King Zog and the Struggle for Stability in Albania*. Boulder: East European Monographs, 1984.

Fuga, Artan. *Mediat dhe Propaganda Totalitare*. Tirana: Monolog, 2010.

Gawrych, George. *The Crescent and the Eagle: Ottoman Rule, Islam and the Albanians, 1874- 1913*. London and New York: I.B.Tauris, 2006.

Gina, Adelina. *Where is my Brother?* North Charleston, South Carolina: Booksurge, 2006.

Gjonça, Arjan. *Communism, Health and Lifestyle: The Paradox of Mortality Transition in Albania 1950-1990*. Westport CT: Greenwood Press, 2001.

Idrizi, Idrit. "Sundimi Komunist në Shqipëri në Periudhën e Vonë të Tij nga Perspektiva e Historisë Kulturore." *Perpjekja*, 32–33 (2014): 70-87.

Ikonomi, Luljeta and Shannon Woodcock. "Imoraliteti në Familje: Nxitja e Ankesave të Grave për të Përforcuar Pushtetin e Partisë në Revolucionin Kulturor Shqiptar." *Perpjekja* 32–33 (2014): 155-182.

Isaku, Vera. *Libër I Hapur: Ruset në Shqipëri*. Tirana: OMSCA-1. 2008.

Kajsiu, Blendi. "Down with Politics! The Crisis of Representation in Post-Communist Albania." *East European Politics & Societies* 24, (2010): 229-253.

Kajsiu, Blendi. *A Discourse Analysis of Corruption: Instituting Neoliberalism Against Corruption in Albania, 1998-2005*. London: Ashgate, 2015.

Klosi, Ardian and Elsa Demo. *Shqipëria Kujton 1944-1991*. Tirana: K & B, 2009.

Kondis, Basil and Eleftheria Manta. *The Greek Minority in Albania: A Documentary Record (1921-1993)*. Thessaloniki: Institute for Balkan Studies, 1994.

Logoreci, Anton. *The Albanians: Europe's Forgotten Survivors*. London: Gollancz, 1977.

Lubonja, Fatos. *Në Vitin e Shtatëmbëdhjetë : Ditar Burgu 1990-1991*. Tirana: Shtëpia Botuese "Marin Barleti," 1994.

Lubonja, Fatos. *Second Sentence: Inside the Albanian Gulag*. Translated by John Hodgson. London: I. B. Tauris, 2009.

Lubonja, Fatos. *False Apocalypse: from Stalinism to Capitalism*. Translated by John Hodgson. London: Istros Books, 2014.

Mëhilli, Elidor. "Defying De-Stalinization: Albania's 1956." *Journal of Cold War Studies* 13 (2011): 4-56.

Musaj, Fatmira. *Gruaja në Shqiperi (1912- 1939)*. Tirana: Akademia e Shkencave të Shqipërisë, 2002.

Musaj, Fatmira, Fatmira Rama and Enriketa Pandelejmoni. "Gender Relations in Albania 1967-2009." In *Gendering Post-Socialist Transition: Studies of Changing Gender Perspectives*, edited by Krassimira Daskalova, 35-63. Vienna: Verlag, 2012.

Musta, Agim. *Prisons of the Prison State*. Tirana: Toena. 2000.

Pearson, Owen. *Albania in the Twentieth Century: Albania and King Zog, Independence, Republic and Monarchy 1908-1939*. London: I.B.Tauris, 2004.

Pearson, Owen. *Albania as Dictatorship and Democracy. From Isolation to the Kosovo War 1946 – 1998*. London: Centre for Albanian Studies, 2006.

Pearson, Owen. *Albania in the Twentieth Century, A History: Vol. 3 1946-1990*. London: I. B. Tauris, 2007.

Pipa, Arshi. *Albanian Stalinism: Ideo-Political Aspects*. New York: Columbia University Press, 1990.

Pllumi, Zef. *Live to tell: A True Story of Religious Persecution in Communist Albania 1944-1951*. New York, Bloomington, Shanghai: iUniverse, 2008.

Prifti, Peter. "The Albanian Women's Struggle for Emancipation." *Southeastern Europe* 2 (1975): 109-129.

Prifti, Peter. *Socialist Albania since 1944: Domestic and Foreign Developments*. Cambridge, Mass: MIT Press. 1978.

Pritchett Post, Susan E. *Women in Modern Albania: Firsthand Accounts of Culture and Conditions from Over 200 Interviews*. Jefferson, North Carolina and London: McFarland & Company, 1998.

Ruches, Pyrrhus J. *Albania's Captives*. Chicago: Argonaut, 1965.

Sandström, Per and Örjan Sjöberg. "Albanian Economic Performance: Stagnation in the 1980s." *Soviet Studies*, 43 (1991): 931-947.

Schwandner-Sievers, Stephanie and Bernd J. Fischer. *Albanian Identities: Myth and History*. London: Hurst, 2002.

Sjöberg, Örjan. *Rural Change and Development in Albania*. Boulder, CO: Westview, 1991.

Stavro, Skendi. *Albania*. Free Europe Committee, Mid-European Studies Center, 1956.

Sulstarova, Enis. *Arratisje nga Lindja: Orientalizmi Shqiptar nga Naimi te Kadareja*. Chapel Hill, NC: Globic Press, 2007.

Vehbiu, Ardia. *Shqipja Totalitare. Tipare të Ligjërimit Publik në Shqipërinë e Viteve 1945-1990*. Tirana: Botime Çabej, 2007.

Vickers, Miranda. *The Albanians: A Modern History*. London: I.B.Tauris, 1995.

Vickers, Miranda and James Pettifer. *Albania: From Anarchy to a Balkan Identity*. London: C. Hurst & Co., 1999.

Vorpsi, Irida. "Fotografia si Mjet i Përhapjes së Propagandës së Emancipimit të Gruas në Shqipërinë Komuniste." *Perpjekja*, 32–33 (2010): 183-204.

Vorpsi, Ornela. *The Country Where No One Ever Dies*. Champaign and London: Dalkey Archive Press, 2009.

Vullnetari, J. and R. King. "Women Here are Like at the Time of Enver [Hoxha]...': Socialist and Post-Socialist Gendered Mobility in Albanian Society." In *Mobilities in Socialist and Post-Socialist States*, edited by Kathy Burrell and Kathrin Hörschelmann, 122-147. London: Palgrave Macmillan, 2014.

Whitaker, Ian. "'A Sack for Carrying Things': The Traditional Role of Women in Northern Albanian Society." *Anthropological Quarterly* 54 (1981): 146-156.

Woodcock, Shannon. "The Absence of Albanian Jokes about Socialism, Or Why Some Dictatorships Are Not Funny." In *The Politics and Aesthetics of Refusal*, edited by Caroline Hamilton, Will Noonan, Michelle Kelly, and Elcine Mines, 51-66. Newcastle, UK: Cambridge Scholars Press, 2007.

Woodcock, Shannon. "Against a Wall: Albania's Women Political Prisoners' Struggle to be Heard." *Cultural Studies Review*, 20 (2014): 39-65.

Woodcock, Shannon and Luljeta Ikonomi. "Imoraliteti në Familje: Nxitja e Ankesave të Grave për të Përforcuar Pushtetin e Partisë në Revolucionin Kulturor Shqiptar" ("'Immorality in the family': The use of women's complaints of rape and incest to strengthen Party control in the Albanian Cultural Revolution") *Perpjekja*, 32-33 (2014): 155-182.

Young, Antonia. *Women Who Become Men: Albanian Sworn Virgins*. Oxford-New York: Berg, 2000.

Socialism and Everyday Life

Adler, Nanci. *Keeping Faith with the Party: Communist Believers Return From the Gulag*. Bloomington: Indiana University Press, 2012.

Ansorg, Leonore and Renate Hürtgen. "The Myth of Female Emancipation: Contradictions in Women's Lives." In *Dictatorship As Experience: Towards a Socio-Cultural History of the GDR* edited by Konrad H. Jarausch, 163-176. New York: Berghahn Books, 1999.

Bardach, Janusz. *Surviving Freedom: After the Gulag.* Oakland: University of California Press, 2003.

Brown, Jeremy and Matthew D. Johnson. *Maoism at the Grassroots: Everyday Life in China's Era of High Socialism.* Cambridge, Massachusetts: Harvard University Press, 2015.

Bucur, Maria, Rayna Gavrilova, Wendy Goldman, Maureen Healy, Kate Lebow and Mark Pittaway. "Six Historians in Search of Alltagsgeschichte." *Aspasia* 3, 2009: 189–212.

Bucur-Deckard, Maria. "Gendering Dissent: Of Bodies and Minds, Survival and Opposition Under Communism." *Oxford Slavonic Papers*, 7–9, 2008: 9-26.

Cormoş, Gratian. *Femei în Infernul Concentrationar din Romania (1945–1989).* Cluj-Napoca: Casa Cărţii de Ştiinţă, 2006.

Dobre, Claudia-Florentina. "Women Remembering Communism in Romania: Former Political Detainees' Perspectives." In *Women and Minorities Archives: Subjects of Archiving*, edited by Kristina Popova and Nurie Muratova, 42-58. vol. 3, Blagoevgrad 2011.

Etkind, Alexander. "Post-Soviet Hauntology: Cultural Memory of the Soviet Terror." *Constellations* 16 (2009): 182-200.

Etkind, Alexander. *Warped Mourning. Stories of the Undead in the Land of the Unburied.* Palo Alto: Stanford University Press, 2013.

Fidelis, Malgorzata. "Recovering Women's Voices in Communist Poland" In *Contesting Archives: Finding Women in the Sources*, edited by Nupur Chaudhuri, Sherry J. Katz and Mary Elizabeth Perry, 107-124. Illinois: University of Illinois Press, 2010.

Fidelis, Malgorzata. *Women, Communism, and Industrialization in Postwar Poland.* New York: Cambridge University Press, 2010.

Figes, Orlando. *The Whisperers: Private Life in Stalin's Russia.* New York: St Martin's Press, 2008.

Fitzpatrick, Sheila and Robert Gellately. *Accusatory Practices: Denunciation in Modern European History, 1789-1989.* Chicago: University of Chicago Press, 1997.

Ghodsee, Kristen. *The Left Side of History: World War II and the Unfulfilled Promise of Communism in Eastern Europe.* Durham: Duke University Press, 2015.

Goven, Joanna. "Gender and Modernism in a Stalinist State." *Social Politics* 9 (2002): 3-28.

Hamilton, Carrie. "Sex, 'Silence', and Audiotape: Listening for Female Same-Sex Desire in Cuba." In *Bodies of Evidence: The Practice of Queer Oral History,* Edited by Nana Alamilla-Boyd and Horacio N. Roque Ramirez, 23-40. Oxford: Oxford University Press, 2012.

Ilic, Melani. *Women in the Stalin Era.* New York: Palgrave Macmillan, 2001.

Ilic, Melanie and Dalia Leinarte. *The Soviet Past in the Post-Socialist Present: Methodology and Ethics in Russian, Baltic and Central European Oral History and Memory Studies.* New York: Routledge, 2015.

Ivanova, Dilyana. *Memories of Everyday Life during Socialism in the Town of Rousse, Bulgaria.* Sofia: The American Research Center in Sofia, 2014.

Kligman, Gail. *The Politics of Duplicity: Controlling Reproduction in Ceausescu's Romania.* Los Angeles: University of California Press, 1998.

Kligman, Gail and Katherine Verdery. *Peasants under Siege: The Collectivization of Romanian Agriculture, 1949-1962.* Princeton: Princeton University Press, 2011.

Luthar, Breda and Maruša Pušnik. *Remembering Utopia: The Culture of Everyday Life in Socialist Yugoslavia.* Washington D.C.: New Academia Publishing, 2010.

Penn, Shana and Jill Massino. *Gender Politics and Everyday Life in State Socialist East and Central Europe.* New York: Palgrave Macmillan, 2009.

Rabikowska, Marta. *The Everyday of Memory: Between Communism and Post-Communism.* Oxford, Berlin: Lang, 2013.

Salecl, Renata. *The Spoils of Freedom: Psychoanalysis and Feminism After the Fall of Socialism.* London and New York: Routledge, 1994.

Shalamov, Varlam. *Kolyma Tales.* New York: Penguin Books, 1994.

Smith, S.A. *The Oxford Handbook of the History of Communism.* Oxford: Oxford University Press, 2014.

Todorova, Maria, Augusta Dimou, and Stefan Troebst. *Remembering Communism: Private and Public Recollections of Lived Experience in Southeast Europe.* Budapest: Central European University Press, 2014.

Oral History, Socialism and Trauma Studies

Améry, Jean. *At the Mind's Limit*. Bloomington: Indiana University Press, 1980.

Alexievitch, Svetlana. *Zinky Boys*. New York: WW Norton & Co, 2008.

Bušková, Kristýna. "Women in Communist Prisons in the 1950s in Czechoslovakia: Understanding Psychological Effects of Political Imprisonment and Ways of Coping using Oral History." *Political Prisoners.eu* website, Accessed January 2, 2016. http://www.politicalprisoners.eu/index.php?id_str=486

Cave, Mark and Stephen M. Sloan. *Listening on the Edge: Oral History in the Aftermath of Crisis*. New York: Oxford University Press, 2014.

Cole, Tim. "(Re)Placing the Past: Spatial Strategies of Retelling Difficult Stories." *Oral History Review* 42 (1) (2015): 1-29.

Herman, Judith L. *Trauma and Recovery: The Aftermath of Violence-From Domestic Abuse to Political Terror*. New York: Basic Books, 1992.

High, Steven. *Beyond Testimony and Trauma: Oral History in the Aftermath of Mass Violence.* Vancouver: UBC Press, 2015.

Khanenko-Friesen, Natalia and Gelinada Grinchenko. *Reclaiming the Personal: Oral History in Post-Socialist Europe*. Toronto: University of Toronto Press, 2015.

Rothschild, Babette. *The Body Remembers: The Psychophysiology of Trauma and Trauma Treatment*. London: W.W. Norton & Co, 2000.

Scarry, Elaine. *The Body in Pain: The Making and Unmaking of the World*. Oxford: Oxford University Press, 1985.

Van der Kolk, Bessel A., Alexander C. McFarlane and Lars Weisaeth. *Traumatic Stress: The Effects of Overwhelming Experience on Mind, Body, and Society.* New York: The Guilford Press, 1996.

Index

abortion, 50-51, 102-104, 146, 161, 166, 199;
    see also contraception
aksion (voluntary labour), 48, 62, 66, 85, 87, 93, 124-25, 131, 145, 170
Albanian economy, 60, 102, 189, 198;
    economic sabotage, 189-190;
    exports, 23, 26-27, 41;
    top politicians using foreing currency, 90, 159, 171
Albanian Cultural and Ideological Revolution, 22, 27, 30, 67, 138,
Albanian elections, 18, 49, 57, 155, 196
Albanian military, 4, 19-21, 46, 48-49, 21, 66-67, 80, 82, 85, 114, 116,
122-25, 131, 179-80
    see also zbor
Alia, Ramiz, 61, 71-72, 101, 104
Alia, Semiramis, 61, 69
Aromanian Albanians, 14, 16, 22-24, 30, 35, 40, 44-45, 111-12, 196;
    shepherding culture, 14, 23-24;   ;
    persecution of, 16, 30, 40, 111-12

Balli Kombëtar (National Front) 3, 15, 137, 158, 196
Ballist
    see Balli Kombëtar (National Front)
Berat, 14, 17-18, 22, 42, 154, 169
Biberaj, Elez, 83-85

     see also religion
Italy, 2-3, 15-16, 20, 55-57, 77, 80, 84, 89, 99, 111, 113, 144, 155, 169, 196

Jokes, 6, 67, 74, 87, 92, 109, 119, 124-25, 133, 137-38, 142-43, 200

Kadare, Ismail, 101, 138
King Zog, 3, 56, 109
kulak, 18, 136-37, 139-40, 159, 196
Kukës, 12, 94-100, 102, 105-8, 150

Land restitution, 73, 159, 199
Legal system, 27, 30, 112, 189, 200;
     Articles of the Penal Code, 143, 189;
     constitution, 30, 48, 140.
     see also propaganda
Lubonja, Fatos, 49
Lushnje, 56, 58, 87

media
     see press
     see television
     see radio
midwifery, 153, 164-66
mosques, 50, 77, 95
     see also Faith Mosque

National Liberation Army, 15
National Liberation Front, 16
National Front
     see Balli Kombëtar (National Front)

Party, The
     see Party of Labor of Albania